This beautifully written, refreshing, and highly intelligent book highlights the much-overlooked human side of teaching. But it's not "fluff." Jonathan Eckert demystifies the complexity of education and shines a spotlight on three necessary teaching elements, helping readers focus on what matters—to change the life of each student.

—Megan Allen
NBCT, Founder, 2010 Florida Teacher of the Year

Leave it to Jonathan Eckert to take a phrase that conjures up the skin crawl of proverbial nails on a chalkboard, use it as a book title, and then convince the reader to embrace it! *Just Teaching* does just that. Although "this book is only about three things," the synergy of well-being, engagement, and feedback as explored in these eight chapters create a powerful design of the essentials to teach *each student* well. Educators who prepare, are prepared, or are preparing to teach will benefit from this thoughtful work of inspiring stories and practical tools.

—P. Ann Byrd
President of CTQ

With *Just Teaching*, Jonathan Eckert has written the right book for the right moment. District and school leaders are seeking coherent ways to frame the important work of academic recovery in a post-pandemic world. Eckert helps us by naming the FEW areas we must prioritize. His straightforward language along with built-in application tools allow even the busiest practitioners to read this book and—more important—use it with their teams in service of supporting students!

—Joan Dabrowski
Chief Academic Officer, Baltimore City Public Schools

The dehumanization of American education on many fronts in the wake of a pandemic has often left teachers and students feeling alienated, like cogs in a broken system that no longer cares. The solution is as it has always been: in the eternity altering spark exchanged between caring teacher and engaged student. In *Just Teaching*, Jonathan Eckert injects new life and passion into this most noble profession, providing simple yet refreshingly creative strategies for engaging students, advancing their well-being, and restoring joy into the schoolhouse. This book will make teachers remember why they love what they do!

—Jay Ferguson
Head of School, Grace Community School, Tyler, TX

What a great book—for those beginning their training and for those in induction programs, as well as for all those already in the classrooms. Eckert reminds us of the power, complexity, simplicity, and joys of teaching. He asks us to savor the time as teachers, and make the experience meaningful to you, your students, and your colleagues. And he backs this with so many ways of thinking and doing that remind us daily of why we all entered this profession: to maximize our impact on others.

—**John Hattie**
Author, VISIBLE LEARNING® series

Jonathan Eckert's joy and admiration for the teaching profession has led him to create a book for teachers that combines a mix of practical advice with life-giving advice for finding the joy in the work. In *Just Teaching: Feedback, Engagement, and Well-Being for Each Student*, he shares advice and research about finding the essential parts of the job while also serving each student. In a time when our schools and communities need teachers more than ever, this book provides a road map for new teachers to begin their profession focusing on the most important aspects of the work and gives experienced teachers space to reclaim their enjoyment of teaching. Woven throughout are practical exercises for reflection, entertaining stories, and research supporting the practices he recommends. "Each educator matters because each student matters" and this book is a road map for making teaching a joy-filled and sustainable profession. And, he wouldn't be a former eduwonk without including a one pager to summarize all this useful advice.

—**JoLisa Hoover**
US Department of Education Teaching
Ambassador Fellow 2008, 2014, 2015

It is easier than ever to feel overwhelmed by the multitude of demands placed on educators. In *Just Teaching*, Jonathan Eckert reminds us that while our plates as teachers may be perennially overfilled, success in the classroom often boils down to a handful of factors that, if approached thoughtfully, can often equal success. Eckert backs these claims up with deep and compelling research and provides his readers with a pile of proven tools for implementing these approaches in their classes. *Just Teaching* is that rare book that seamlessly blends scholarship, philosophy, and practicality and will be on my list to buy for almost every teacher I know.

—**Matthew Johnson**
Author, *Answers to Your Biggest Questions
About Teaching Middle and High School ELA*

Jonathan Eckert delivers a powerhouse book that every educator (and parent) needs now. Students are struggling like never before, and Eckert's *Just Teaching* clearly explains why every child must be seen, heard, and loved and how to get there. This book is an urgent must read.

—David Magee
Bestselling author (*Dear William*) and a creator of the William Magee Institute for Student Wellbeing at the University of Mississippi

Jonathan Eckert is a rare jewel among teacher educators today. He brings together a deep understanding of educational research, of practical classroom realities, and of the love of Christ. In *Just Teaching*, he draws on these understandings to pull us all back to the core of all teaching and learning: feedback, engagement, wellness. New and veteran educators will find this book revitalizing.

—Renee Moore
NBCT, BOD Vice Chair, Center for Teaching Quality

Just Teaching is a must read for any teacher looking to build a strong classroom community where all voices are heard, students connect with the teacher and with each other, and take control of their learning. This book is needed today. In the state of our current world, students may feel more disconnected from each other face-to-face than ever. The truth is that no matter how much the teaching profession changes and evolves, the students who sit in front of us just want us to connect with and understand them. In this book, Jonathan Eckert brings us back to the heart and soul of teaching and how to rehumanize the classroom experience.

—Serena Pariser
Author, *Answers to Your Biggest Questions About Creating a Dynamic Classroom*

At a time when parents are more engaged than ever in their children's education, Eckert offers practical strategies that parents and educators alike can embrace to help each child thrive in school. This book builds on its foundational advice to center love and relationships in a student's academic journey, and it models those central elements through anecdotes, tools, and resources to help students meet their goals.

—Jocelyn Pickford
Senior Affiliate, HCM Strategists

Jonathan Eckert is one of my go-to sources of wisdom, as I have grown to trust him deeply by observing how he leads his family, his classroom, and his fellow faculty. He is an educator of educators. If you have been challenged by the new landscape of education, you will find an incredible guide in Jonathan Eckert and this much-needed resource! Please read it and share it with everyone in your field.

—Jonathan Pokluda
Bestselling author, host of the *Becoming Something* podcast, and lead pastor of Harris Creek

This book reminds me so much of the work of Marva Collins and Gloria Ladson-Billings, two of my greatest SHEroes. Both felt that teaching was beyond curriculum, but it was a work of the heart. Teaching involves the heart of the teacher connecting with the heart of each student they may encounter. Jonathan Eckert's book provides a very practical way for all teachers to learn the skill of seeing each student for who they are and reaching them where they are, so that the classroom becomes a cocoon for all children to develop into beings who can soar to the greatest heights.

—Anika Prather
Director of High Quality Curriculum and Instruction at the Institute for Education Policy at Johns Hopkins University and Lecturer at Howard University

Just Teaching is refreshingly honest, clear, and heart centered. Reading Jonathan Eckert's stories and using his tools is an opportunity for all of us to bring joy back into the classroom. *Just Teaching* simplifies the complex issues so we can focus on what is most essential to our well-being and the success of our students.

—Carol Pelletier Radford
Author, *Teaching With Light: Ten Lessons for Finding Wisdom, Balance, and Inspiration*

Student engagement is critical to learning but too many students are disengaged, and studies show an alarming drop in student engagement in advanced grade levels. Jonathan Eckert combines a thoughtful analysis of the root causes of this challenge with highly practical solutions for educators to be more successful in connecting with and engaging each individual student. Eckert shares a compelling vision for educators, parents, and leaders at the system level to better support and engage each individual student in their learning journey.

—Kristan Van Hook
Senior Vice President of Policy at the National Institute for Excellence in Teaching

Just Teaching

Just Teaching

FEEDBACK, ENGAGEMENT, & WELL-BEING FOR EACH STUDENT

JONATHAN ECKERT

FOR INFORMATION:

Corwin
A SAGE Company
2455 Teller Road
Thousand Oaks, California 91320
(800) 233-9936
www.corwin.com

SAGE Publications Ltd.
1 Oliver's Yard
55 City Road
London EC1Y 1SP
United Kingdom

SAGE Publications India Pvt. Ltd.
B 1/I 1 Mohan Cooperative Industrial Area
Mathura Road, New Delhi 110 044
India

SAGE Publications Asia-Pacific Pte. Ltd.
18 Cross Street #10-10/11/12
China Square Central
Singapore 048423

President: Mike Soules
Vice President and
  Editorial Director: Monica Eckman
Executive Editor: Tori Mello Bachman
Content Development Editor: Sharon Wu
Editorial Assistant: Nancy Chung
Project Editor: Amy Schroller
Copy Editor: Erin Livingston
Typesetter: C&M Digitals (P) Ltd.
Cover Designer: Gail Buschman
Marketing Manager: Margaret O'Connor

Printed in Canada

Library of Congress Cataloging-in-Publication Data

Names: Eckert, Jonathan, author.

Title: Just teaching : feedback, engagement, and well-being for each student / Jonathan Eckert.

Description: Thousand Oaks, California : Corwin, [2023] | Series: Corwin teaching essentials ; Volume 1 | Includes bibliographical references and index.

Identifiers: LCCN 2022047878 | ISBN 9781071886588 (paperback) | ISBN 9781071903711 (epub) | ISBN 9781071903704 (epub) | ISBN 9781071903698 (pdf)

Subjects: LCSH: Teacher effectiveness. | Feedback (Psychology) | Motivation in education. | Well-being. | Teacher-student relationships. | Teaching—Psychological aspects.

Classification: LCC LB1025.3 .E283 2023 | DDC 371.102—dc23/eng/20221013
LC record available at https://lccn.loc.gov/2022047878

This book is printed on acid-free paper.

23 24 25 26 27 10 9 8 7 6 5 4 3 2

Contents

For the eight teaching tools and other resources related to *Just Teaching*, please visit the companion website at **resources.corwin.com/justteaching.**

Acknowledgments

Last week, my 19-year-old son led our whole family across Spain—from Madrid to Barcelona to Pamplona. I wish that I would have acquired the writing skills of Ernest Hemingway by following in his footsteps so that I could do justice to the people who have made this book possible, but unfortunately, that does not seem to be how this works. I will do my best after 26 years of learning from some of the best educators in the world to communicate my gratitude, but I am certain I will leave many people out because you have become so much a part of me and my teaching practice.

To all the educators who are named and unnamed in the book, thank you for your examples and willingness to share your work. Good ideas in education come from real schools and classrooms, and I would not have any to share if you did not make your practice public. Beyond sharing your practice, you also shared your expertise. I am particularly grateful for Jolene Bruce, Crystal Chapman, Lynda Copple, McKenna Ferrell, Africa Jones, Katie Kilpatrick, and Kathleen Peercy—all amazing educators who gave me excellent feedback throughout my writing process. To Ann Byrd and Alesha Daughtrey at the Center for Teaching Quality, thank you for your leadership, constantly reframing my thinking, and continuing to allow me to work with some of the best teachers and administrators across the country.

Our team at Baylor University is a tremendous blessing. To my K–12 colleagues who have joined with me these last three years—Bradley Carpenter, Herb Cox, and Angela Urick—I am so excited about what we are building in educational leadership. To our MA and EdD students, thank you for growing with us—your examples populate these pages. You do the hard work of leading schools every day, and it is an honor to walk alongside you. To our Baylor Center for School Leadership team—Erik Ellefsen, Stacey Lumley, and Matt Thomas—thanks for all the work we do together. Erik, thanks for over 20 years of dreams, calls, and shared life—the section in Chapter 8 does not do you justice, but it was the best I could do. Stacey, thanks for trying to keep us close to sane. Matt, thanks for all the conversations, feedback, friendship, and road trips to schools. Thanks to Lynda and Robert Copple for the endowed gift that makes our work possible and for your constant encouragement.

The dedication is to my kids this time. Thanks for your encouragement, for your endless education examples, and for being the best kids anyone could ever have. Each one of you is a gift. While the dedication is to our kids, every dedication should really be to my wife, Carolyn. I am so grateful that we get to walk through life together. Thanks for loving me, for telling me when there is something in my teeth, and for planning adventures so I do not work too much.

The evidence of just teaching is everywhere. Just teachers leave indelible marks on us—we are their "unsigned manuscripts." Our son can lead us all over Spain because of Señora Landon, his high school Spanish teacher who inspired him to study abroad in Madrid. This book is my offering as the "unsigned manuscript" of so many teachers. This is the power of just teachers.

Publisher's Acknowledgments

Corwin gratefully acknowledges the contributions of the following reviewers:

Alice Braunstein
Special Education Teacher, Staten Island, NY

Jigisha Vyas
Instructional Coach, Fair Lawn, NJ

Serena Pariser
Author and Educational Consultant, St. Louis Park, MN

Leslie Goines
School Counselor, Metropolis, IL

Renee Schultz
Elementary Teacher, Waldwick, NJ

About the Author

Jonathan Eckert was a public school teacher outside of Chicago and Nashville for 12 years. He earned his doctorate in education at Vanderbilt University and served as a U.S. Department of Education Teaching Ambassador Fellow in both the Bush and Obama administrations. Currently, he is the Lynda and Robert Copple Chair and Professor of Educational Leadership at Baylor University, where he supports leaders through the Center for School Leadership. Leading professional learning across the country, he catalyzes teaching and leading for each student. He is the author of *The Novice Advantage* and *Leading Together*.

To Ben, Sarah, and Grace and three people they identified as just teachers:

Ms. Bostrom, Ms. Moos, and Ms. Garner.

So grateful they could have picked many more.

Prologue

"We need to 'decomplexify' this for educators."

A senior official at the U.S. Department of Education said this about her desire to make sensible policies for teachers. While I appreciated her sentiment, I could not miss the irony of the fact that in trying to communicate this notion in her own bureaucratic way, she chose the word *decomplexify*—a word that does not exist in standard dictionaries.

She could have just said *simplify*.

Teachers and administrators do not need bureaucrats to complicate their work with terms like *decomplexify*. Now more than ever, we need elegant solutions that address the complexity of the world in ways that do not overwhelm us. So many conversations begin, "There are no silver bullets, but . . ." What if there is a silver bullet? We can create silver bullets—but every mold has to look a little different because each student we serve is uniquely gifted with skills, experiences, and opportunities. In other words, we don't serve *all* students; we serve *each* student.

> We don't serve *all* students; we serve *each* student.

This book is grounded in decades of research and experiences that demonstrate that there has never been a better time to be in education. We know more about how people learn, have more tools to support that learning, and have more vehicles for educational delivery than at any point in the history of the world.

Teaching is the profession that makes all others possible, but sometimes we make it overly complicated.

We need to stop performing, entertaining, judging, stressing, enabling, and dictating.

We need to become better learners—better listeners, readers, coaches, and truth tellers.

To become better learners as educators and students, we need three things: feedback, engagement, and well-being. At its essence, learning is contingent upon these three components that conveniently form the acronym FEW. In times of complexity, we need to focus on a few ideas. Each student deserves educators who support their learning in these three ways.

The title of the book, *Just Teaching*, has two purposes. First, teaching should not be overwhelming. Teaching is the most life-giving work that we do because it is essential for developing thriving human beings. Together, we will break down what is essential and can become more life-giving. We do not have to respond to feeling overwhelmed by working even harder. Second, I am devastated when I hear teachers refer to themselves as "just teachers," as if they are powerless and have no status. What if we could turn the meaning of that phrase upside-down and claim its redemptive power? "Just teachers" care for each student. Teachers who are just cultivate freedom and flourishing. "Just teaching" clarifies and elevates the essential work we do as educators.

The solution is for *each* student. To get to the solution, we have to stop thinking about *all* students as if students are faceless components of an amorphous blob. We must move past thinking in subgroups, categories, stereotypes, and caricatures. We need to see, hear, love, and respect each student.

Well-being, Engagement, and Feedback

To fully address the FEW ideas in the book, we have to reverse the acronym. We cannot get to feedback without first attending to well-being. Well-being can be part of a virtuous or vicious cycle. The virtuous cycle looks like this: If administrators are physically, psychologically, emotionally, socially, and spiritually well, then they can serve teachers effectively. If teachers are well, they can serve students well. If students are well, they flourish, and the school flourishes and supports the well-being of the community. Unfortunately, much of what we have seen in recent years has looked like the opposite of this, which is a vicious cycle.

Well-being is the foundation on which we build learning. Meaningful learning does not occur when a student is in a trauma-induced state of fight, flight, freeze, or appease. If the amygdala senses danger, those are the four options it gives students. This has always been true, but it

FIGURE 0.1 Just Teaching "Decomplexified"

FEEDBACK, ENGAGEMENT, & WELL-BEING

WELL-BEING
PURPOSE-DRIVEN FLOURISHING

FEEDBACK
PURPOSE-DRIVEN
WISDOM FOR GROWTH

ENGAGEMENT
CONTENT, CONSOLIDATION,
COLLABORATION, CREATION

becomes abundantly clear in times of significant disruption. The pandemic thrust most students and educators worldwide into completely new territory that was isolating and exhausting. If well-being is not supported, then we never get to meaningful engagement or assessment and feedback on student work.

Engagement has been missing as well. During significant disruptions caused by pandemics or natural disasters, many students cannot access online resources due to insufficient hardware, software, or instruction. That makes engagement impossible. Lack of engagement can be more subtle and insidious as well. As students have been forced to increasingly embrace screens, software engineers are constantly competing for their attention while students try to do their homework. This is a rigged game with billions of dollars pouring into the attention economy that is rapidly reducing students' cognitive endurance.

Feedback flows from meaningful engagement because engagement should lead to deliberate practice. Deliberate practice requires feedback from others for improvement. This should be the objective for all educators because it is how we create lifelong learners. We come alongside students to help them become the best, most complete versions of themselves. We do that by providing scaffolding and challenging learning experiences that we assess with clear-eyed honesty and provide feedback on how students can improve. We also need feedback for ourselves as educators because feedback is the cornerstone of deliberate practice. The FEW ideas described here are not linear but should reinforce each other. In other words, feedback should enhance engagement and support well-being so that continuous improvement occurs.

Who Should Use This Book?

Don't simply read this book. Use this book. Although I wrote this book with aspiring and practicing classroom teachers in mind, administrators, policymakers, and parents may find this book useful to develop solutions that work for each student. This book is only about three things. If you are looking for simple, direct approaches to finding solutions to complex issues in education, this book is for you. In a world of ever-changing priorities, conditions, and strategies, you can use this book to return to the basics of what works for students. This book will simplify your approach to education in a way that will unleash your power for creative problem solving.

Instead of merely unleashing your own creativity, use this with a team. If we do this creative work in teams of teachers, administrators, and parents, we can show policymakers how to solve seemingly intractable problems such as apathy, distraction, underachievement, inequity, and lack of purpose. A single teacher cannot do this work alone. We need administrators and teachers to lead this work together in partnership with the families and communities they serve.

How Will This Book Help Us Develop Solutions?

This book is divided into four parts. Chapter 1 and Chapter 8 focus on each student and each educator. Focusing on each student makes teaching infinitely interesting and brings meaning to what we do. Given the tyranny of the urgency that educators face every day, each chapter will begin with key takeaways. This could help in three ways. First, by reading these boxes, you could "read" this entire book in about eight minutes. Obviously, you will miss a lot of nuance and practical application, but you will have a sense of the book. Second, you can use these boxes to identify areas of the chapter where you want to focus your time, as the boxes follow the order of the chapters. Third, you could use the boxes to review key ideas when you revisit a chapter after an initial read. Regardless of how you use these boxes or this book, I hope they are helpful.

At the end of each chapter, you will find one tool that will be a component of a solution to develop thriving students. The point of the tool is for you to do the hard work (preferably with others) of moving toward solutions—not talking about a possibility, considering an improvement, or perseverating on what a solution might be. At the end of each chapter, you will start doing the work. In the final chapter, you will bring all the tools together. You can also download each tool as fillable PDFs from the website (http://justschools.net) if you would prefer to use them that way.

Sandwiched between Chapters 1 and 8 will be Part I. Well-being, Part II. Engagement, and Part III. Feedback. Part I addresses how we connect with other human beings by focusing on their basic needs first. Simple strategies rooted in complex truths about students and educators animate this section. Part II tackles the four *C*s of student engagement: content, consolidation, collaboration, and creation. Specifically, teachers look at themselves and move beyond content presentation to deeper levels of engagement through a laser focus on each student. Part III explores feedback based on authentic assessments and performance tasks. In this section, assessment becomes a celebration of learning, and feedback is life-giving for the giver and receiver.

If you are interested in the most effective ways to serve each student based on the best research on how students learn and the wisdom of thousands of educators with the best tools available in a way that focuses what we do as educators, let's go. By the end of this book, you will be "just teaching" in the best sense of the phrase.

Each Before All

We can't miss the tree for the forest.

Just Teaching

Chapter 1 "Decomplexified"

- Schools are better when educators move from serving some students to serving all students. Schools are great when they move from serving all students to seeing each student.

- To see each student well, we need honest, hard, respectful conversations about improvement grounded in relationships.

- To serve each student, educators must attend to a FEW ideas: feedback, engagement, and well-being.

- Personalized learning happens best through relationships. To build those relationships, we need to
  - be genuinely curious,
  - make time, especially when it is not convenient (e.g., use the 2x10), and
  - demonstrate love to cultivate joy.

- Like sequoia redwoods, we grow best when we grow in networks of rooted relationships.

Each Student

Anthony[1] was living in the homeless shelter with his mom and brother. He had changed schools six times in four years, and he entered my fifth-grade classroom in October. He was all of five feet tall and did

---

[1] All student names will be pseudonyms to protect privacy.

not weigh 70 pounds. He was constantly hungry, and his pants were always a couple of inches too short. Although he was bright, there were significant holes in what he had learned because he had shifted schools so many times. These holes led to a lack of confidence and a tendency for him to withdraw. Maybe during the first or second school transition Anthony had the energy to try to engage in new classroom contexts and friends, but by move six he was not interested in making new friends, taking new risks, or trusting anyone.

Sadly, his story of homelessness is the story of 1.36 million students in the United States (Meltzer et al., 2019). Situations such as Anthony's become even more challenging when we throw in cascading and pervasive trauma—pandemics, fires, hurricanes, and racial injustice. These are the issues that students, families, teachers, and administrators face every day. These issues make educating students so challenging. Every context is different. Every community is different. Every school is different. Every classroom is different. Every child is different. If you have ever taught middle school students, you also know that every child can be different every hour of the day, depending on which way the hormonal winds are blowing.

This is not a bad thing. This is what makes teaching fascinating for educators—people who study students and not simply a subject. Any experienced educator can tell you that teaching is about so much more than content. The complexity of each individual and what is involved in communicating with them is what enthralls great teachers. In fact, there are six frames of interaction between two people (Cooper & Simonds, 2007).

1) There is my version of me.

2) There is my version of you.

3) There is my version of how you see me.

4) There is your version of you.

5) There is your version of me.

6) There is your version of how I see you.

For some high school teachers, multiply that by 200 students and you get 1,200 frames of interaction daily.

200 students × 6 frames = 1,200 frames/day

As educators, we cannot think of an individual student as a faceless member of a class, race, ethnicity, or gender, much less a number on a standardized test. Each student is uniquely gifted with talents, abilities, and interests. We have to give each student feedback on their engaged learning, which can only happen when we have addressed their well-being. Like Anthony, each student is burdened or blessed by particular formative experiences that create opportunities or obstacles. We can't miss the tree for the forest of students that surround them.

What We Know: From Some to All to Each

Through the Baylor Center for School Leadership, we have talked to thousands of educators around the world over the past few years to determine how they are serving students through some of the most significant education disruptions in history. Far from developing new approaches or designing innovative apps, we are seeing a return to fundamentals. As good coaches know, when adversity and complexity arise, you take the team back to the fundamentals of what breeds success.

Some to All: An Outdated Model

Over the last few decades in education, we have moved from an emphasis on some students to an emphasis on all students. When I first started teaching, my students' test scores were reported as an aggregated grade-level average. Districts near mine were notorious for scheduling field trips on state testing days for students with special needs or other students who might bring down the average performance of their schools. In 2001, the reauthorization of the Elementary and Secondary Education Act declared that as a nation, we would focus on each student. Over two decades later, we know that this did not really happen. How did a law that seemingly no one would oppose based on its name—No Child Left Behind—fail to focus our attention on each child? How did the law literally and figuratively become a four-letter word—NCLB—with remarkably negative connotations for so many? Based on my experience as a teacher and at the U.S. Department of Education in both the Bush and Obama administrations, the emphasis on standardizing accountability for complex outcomes fell victim to Campbell's Law: "The more any quantitative social indicator is used for social decision-making, the more subject it will be to corruption pressures and the more apt it will be to distort and corrupt the social processes it is intended to monitor" or, stated more simply, "When a measure becomes a target, it ceases to become a good measure" (Hess, 2018).

While there were flaws in its design and implementation, NCLB did move our collective attention from an aggregated average of all students' performance to reporting based on subcategories, particularly race/ethnicity, with requirements that we had to assess nearly every student. Schools could no longer hide behind the performance of most students; they had to account for the performance of each subgroup.

While NCLB might have moved us from the performance of some students to most students, NCLB never really moved us toward an emphasis on each student. In many places, students were reduced to reading and math test scores and graduation rates. We looked at students who were on the bubble of proficiency in math and reading, referring to them as "bubble kids," to see if we could give them some additional support to push them over the proficiency standard to meet the 2013 goal of all students at grade-level proficiency in reading and math. The measure became the target and all that mattered. Our focus became myopic and distorted. When states dropped writing tests or reduced testing in science or social studies in Grades 3–8, we stopped teaching those subjects as anything more than ways to improve reading and math scores. Instead of *doing* science in elementary and middle school, we began to use science to teach nonfiction reading strategies.

Just this past year, I studied a relatively high-performing prekindergarten (PreK) through Grade 8 urban school.

Pause a moment: When you hear the phrase "relatively high-performing urban school," what comes to mind?

You are probably thinking of predominantly Black and Brown students who are scoring better than their peers in math and reading. Right? You would be right. Unfortunately, these kinds of labels reduce students to their race/ethnicity and test scores. In this school, kindergarteners sat at attention with their hands folded on top of their desks. In the kindergarten room, there were no spaces for centers and no carpet for morning meetings—just students sitting in rows trying to focus on their teacher. All the other K–8 classrooms looked the same. There were no art rooms, music rooms, or science labs. In fact, this was the first year that middle school students were receiving any significant instruction in science. The laser focus was entirely on raising math and reading scores as measured by standardized achievement tests.

The focus was not on each student. Each student's test score as a component of the average test scores of the school seemed to be all that mattered. If that is the primary value of a student, then we miss the mark on our purpose as educators: to serve whole human beings so that each one can flourish. When we focus on test scores, even each student's test scores, we disembody learning. We suck the soul from education.

All to Each: Cultivating Whole Individuals

Life-giving teaching flows through relationships. These relationships should be grounded in truth and love because we have to meet each student where they are. We must have conversations that are

1) honest

2) hard

3) respectful conversations

4) focused on improvement

5) grounded in relationship (Eckert, 2018).

We have to tell the truth well to each student. We do not love a student well when we sugarcoat the truth, omit the truth, or even lie to make them feel better about a performance that does not meet the mark or maximize their potential. Research shows that high school students whose teachers have higher expectations for them are three times more likely to graduate from college than students with similar grades whose teachers hold them to lower expectations (Boser et al., 2014). Love is having a hard conversation with a student about where they need to grow. Love is giving meaningful feedback on a piece of writing that is not where it needs to be. Love is telling a parent that a student is not ready to move on to the next unit or concept and will need more time at lunch or additional support to achieve prerequisite skills or knowledge. Love requires us to be truthful—even and especially when it is hard.

Parents and students cannot hear truth if we do not ground that truth in love and relationships. Our relationships must be about more than simply academics. At its core, the relationship between teacher and student is grounded in truth and love, which are expressed in three primary concepts: feedback, engagement, and well-being (FEW). To make this easy, we need to remember a FEW things (see Figure 1.1).

- **Feedback** for improvement is the ultimate goal of deliberate practice (Ericsson et al., 1993), which is how we get better.

- Feedback is only possible if there is deep, purposeful **engagement** (Dweck, 2006).

- Engagement only occurs if educator and student **well-being** are addressed (Harding et al., 2019).

These FEW ideas work best when each student is seen and known deeply by others. A quotation often attributed to Yale professor James Comer states, "No significant learning can occur without significant relationship." Some have questioned this. They cite examples such as Khan Academy. Can't technology mediate learning? Do we really need a relationship to learn? Listening to Sal Khan explain math makes me feel like I can achieve mathematical greatness, but I do not have a relationship, right? Khan Academy and many other learning platforms can facilitate

FIGURE 1.1   Feedback, Engagement, and Well-being
for Each Student

FEEDBACK, ENGAGEMENT, & WELL-BEING

WELL-BEING
PURPOSE-DRIVEN FLOURISHING

FEEDBACK
PURPOSE-DRIVEN
WISDOM FOR GROWTH

ENGAGEMENT
CONTENT, CONSOLIDATION,
COLLABORATION, CREATION

SCAN THE QR CODE
FOR A FILLABLE PDF

learning, but having an effective educator who connects with each student is the only way to produce significant learning that addresses feedback, engagement, and well-being. Sal Khan can help me understand calculus, but he cannot attend to my well-being or give me meaningful feedback beyond whether I answered correctly through an automated process. Feedback, engagement, and well-being are job security for good educators and hope for society, as we do not learn to enact virtues from Khan Academy. As Martin Luther King Jr. famously said, "Intelligence plus character; that is the true goal of education." We develop that character through meaningful feedback, engagement, and attention to well-being.

We cannot let this overwhelm us. In fact, by focusing on these three essential ideas, we make teaching more "effortless." James McKeown (2014), in his first book, *Essentialism*, helps us identify our big rocks. He uses the image of placing rocks in a jar. If we fill the jar up with all the tiny rocks (the inconsequential things in our lives) and then try to add our big rocks (those things that matter most), then we cannot make the big rocks fit (see Figure 1.2, Jar A). If we start with the big rocks and then add the small rocks, everything can fit (see Jar B). This makes a lot of intuitive and spatial sense. However, McKeown came to acknowledge that even if we eliminate all the small rocks, sometimes we cannot make the big rocks all fit (see Jar C).

FIGURE 1.2   *Essentialism and the Need for Effortless*

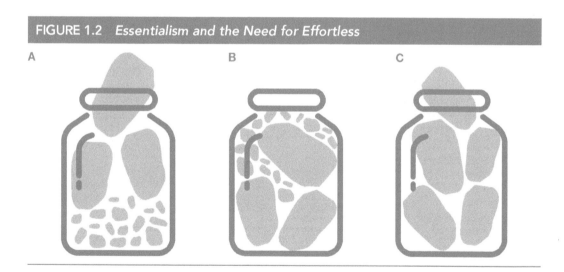

To address the overwhelming number of big rocks, he wrote *Effortless* (2021). The basic premise is this: "What could happen in your life if the easy but pointless things became harder and the essential things became easier?" This is the whole idea of FEW (see boxed text). By focusing on these three big rocks, and finding their life-giving qualities for teachers and students, we can energize and invigorate our work. The reality of the need to reach each student is what makes teaching infinitely interesting and why teaching is the profession that makes all others possible. This is why education will never be teacher-proof.

Just teaching should not be exhausting. "Burnout is not a badge of honor" (McKeown, 2021, p. 7). Here are a few lessons we can apply from *Effortless* (2021) to just teaching. Figure 1.3 and the table below represent what we think, do, and get when we move from exhausting teaching toward life-giving teaching. I do not believe teaching will ever be effortless, but the effort can be life-giving. We can apply these lessons to leadership as well.

FIGURE 1.3   Exhausting vs. Life-giving

	EXHAUSTING	LIFE-GIVING
Think	Anything worth doing takes tremendous effort *(leading, teaching, learning)*	The most essential things can be the easiest ones *(FEW)*
Do	Try too hard: complexify, micromanage, overthink *(alone)*	Find the easier path *(care for self, engage others, eliminate steps, focus on joy)*
Get	Burnout and none of the results you want *(no FEW)*	The right results without burning out *(FEW)*

In the left column, exhausting leadership and teaching are lonely, make everything hard, and result in burnout. The exhausting approach turns leading and teaching into micromanaging and overthinking because we are focused on ourselves and somehow believe that hard work is more meaningful. If we take the life-giving approach, we focus on what matters most—FEW. We simplify by eliminating anything that distracts us as we engage others in ways that bring us joy while we also care for ourselves. If we do this well, we are energized by the work and we get better results than what we might have even imagined on our own.

In 2008, along with a teacher from Tunisia, I was the keynote speaker on teacher quality at a G7 (group of seven largest economies in the world) Broader Middle East–North African Summit in Muscat, Oman. During the summit, I had a conversation with a senior official from the Institute for Education Sciences, the research wing of the U.S. Department of Education, who told me that the topic of teacher quality would be irrelevant within a decade, because, in his words, "curriculum and instruction would be teacher-proofed." He believed students would receive personalized learning through one-to-one digital technology interfaces by 2018. We have seen how woefully short his predictions fell when we were forced into versions of this digital interface for curriculum delivery in 2020 during the COVID-19 pandemic.

Part of the reason I teach is because I believe people such as this senior official are wrong. Each educator matters *because* each student matters. A 2019 study of more than 3,000 students and 1,000 educators found that higher levels of teacher well-being are associated with higher levels of student well-being. Students have higher levels of connection and belonging at their schools when their teachers are well (Harding et al., 2019)—another reason education will never be teacher-proof.

Education is one of, if not the most, human endeavors that we undertake. Anyone who has spent any time in a classroom knows that good teaching is living and learning from and with each other.

Personalized Learning Through Relationships

Never has the need for personalized learning been greater. Even before the world shifted in response to a pandemic, organizations such as Summit Learning have been attempting to personalize learning. With engineering and financial support from the Chan Zuckerberg Initiative, Summit Learning has been working to find ways to focus on the needs of each student. Using the engineering expertise of Facebook and over $140,000,000 of support has engendered optimism about truly personalized learning (Mathewson, 2020). In many ways, there has never been a better time to be in education. We know more about how students learn, we have more instructional tools, and we are educating more students than we ever have.

However, that is not how it feels to most educators. Initiatives such as Summit Learning also engender fear and concern over quality, student screen time, and data privacy (Mathewson, 2020). Additionally, 55% of teachers do not want their own children to follow them into the profession (Phi Delta Kappan, 2019), and teacher morale hit all-time lows in 2020–2021, with nearly 85% of teachers reporting lower morale than before the pandemic (Will, 2021).

Chronic absenteeism is at 22% (Dorn et al., 2021). That rate is more than double pre-pandemic rates.

Health insurance claims for mental health doubled among teenagers from 13 to 18 years old during the pandemic, according to an analysis of a database of 32 billion health insurance claims. Researchers examined 2 billion claims filed on people from birth to 22 years old. The three primary conditions were anxiety, depression, and adjustment disorders. Drug overdoses among 13- to 18-year-olds also doubled (FAIR Health, 2021).

Students are lonely. As we age, loneliness increases the risk for early mortality as much as smoking 15 cigarettes per day (Holt-Lunstad et al., 2015).

In an August 26, 2021, column titled, "The Real Reason Kids Don't Like School" for *The Atlantic,* Arthur Brooks (2021) cited several studies that identify challenges with schools in general. In a study of more than 21,000 high school students, almost 80% report that they are "stressed," almost 70% report they are "bored," and nearly 75% of them self-reported feeling negative (Moeller et al., 2020). Brooks argues that the primary reason for this is that students are lonely and need a friend (see box).

Since 2009, the Gallup Student Poll has collected responses from over six million students in Grades 5–12 from more than 8,000 schools across 1,400 districts. The survey tracks hope, engagement, belonging, and social-emotional learning of students. The survey uses nine items to examine student engagement and compares them across grade levels. Figure 1.4 shows findings from 2016 when the results were broken out by grade level and item. There are significant declines in every area in Grades 5–8 but having a "best friend at school" is the highest-rated area for engagement at school in both areas.

FIGURE 1.4   2016 Gallup Student Poll Engagement Items (% Strongly Agree)

ITEMS	GRADE 5	GRADE 11
At this school, I get to do what I do best every day.	35	17
My teachers make me feel that my schoolwork is important.	66	28
I feel safe in this school.	62	30
I have fun at school.	47	16
I have a best friend at school.	84	57
In the last seven days, someone has told me I have done good work at school.	50	30
In the last seven days, I have learned something interesting at school.	59	32
The adults at my school care about me.	67	24
I have at least one teacher who makes me excited about the future.	71	44

https://news.gallup.com/poll/1612/education.aspx

If student engagement and satisfaction with schools are related, then more recent Gallup data are cause for concern. In surveys of the public, Gallup has found that satisfaction with schools, in general, has declined through the pandemic (see Figure 1.5).

FIGURE 1.5   Gallup K–12 U.S. Satisfaction Survey 1999–2021

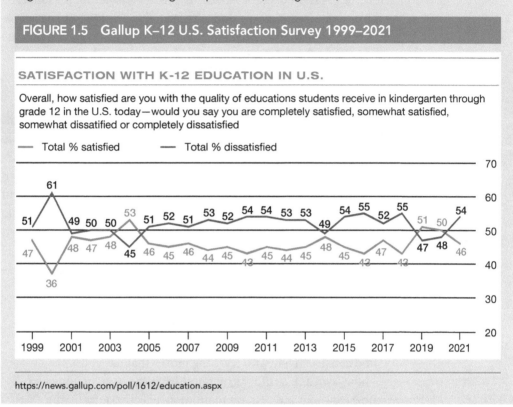

SATISFACTION WITH K-12 EDUCATION IN U.S.

Overall, how satisfied are you with the quality of educations students receive in kindergarten through grade 12 in the U.S. today—would you say you are completely satisfied, somewhat satisfied, somewhat dissatified or completely dissatisfied

— Total % satisfied   — Total % dissatisfied

https://news.gallup.com/poll/1612/education.aspx

So, what is real? Is this the best time to be an educator or a student? Or is it the worst?

Through our work at the Baylor Center for School Leadership (with over 600 schools over the last two years), my colleagues and I have come to realize that meeting the needs of each student remains challenging— maybe more challenging than ever—but it is not impossible. Holistic, personalized learning is best mediated through deep relationship. Education is more than accruing skills and knowledge for an economic outcome. Through significant educational disruption, we have learned that being present and in relationship matters for each student. Learning in-person increases student morale (Kurtz, 2021) and student achievement (Texas Education Agency, 2021). Having teachers who care improves student outcomes (Smylie et al., 2020), and this is true at all educational levels. In a study of intermediate grades, teachers who intentionally use techniques to establish, maintain, and restore relationships enhance student academic engagement by 33% and reduce disruptive behavior by 75% (Cook,

Coco et al., 2018). College graduates who strongly agreed that they have a professor who cared about them as a person were 1.9 times more likely to be engaged at work and 1.7 times more likely to be thriving in their well-being (Matson & Clark, 2020). This is the essence of personalized learning—being seen, known, and appreciated as an individual by people who attend to student well-being and student engagement and provide meaningful feedback for growth.

What Works in Real Schools: Know Each Student

Before we can address our FEW ideas, we have to know each student. This lies at the center of equitable, just teaching practice. At a Visible Learning Conference in 2018, Zaretta Hammond said, "Equity is reducing the predictability of who fails." We should not be able to walk into a classroom, look at individual students or at a group of students, and identify who is most likely to fail. We used to refer to these students as *at-risk*—a term that minimizes the cultural capital and assets each student brings to the classroom. Equity is giving each student what they need to be successful. This requires culturally responsive teaching, as defined by Hammond (2015):

> An educator's ability to recognize students' cultural displays of learning and meaning making and respond positively and constructively with teaching moves that use cultural knowledge as a scaffold to connect what the student knows to new concepts and content to promote effective information processing. All the while, the educator understands the importance of being in a relationship and having a social-emotional connection to the student in order to create a safe space for learning. (p. 15)

To be culturally responsive, each student must be seen and known. This requires building, cultivating, and sustaining relationships with students. As educators, we are not simply responding to culture, we are responding to individuals. For example, Jamal, an excellent high school student, began to struggle academically. His grades started dropping and he appeared increasingly tired and disengaged. A teacher asked him what was going on and then problem solved with a school administrator and the family during a home visit. The family was trying to run all their electrical devices from one working outlet, and their water heater and stove were not working. The administrator who lived in the same neighborhood called in a few favors and personally installed a new stove and water heater and addressed the electrical issues. Jamal's performance at school improved dramatically.

Most instances are less dramatic than Jamal's example. Teachers daily see students' needs and do what they can to meet them. Whether it is an email home, keeping a box of cereal in the room for students who missed breakfast, or identifying a learning need, great teachers are continually seeing and responding to student needs.

Educators cannot solve every challenge that students face, but we can elicit students' stories in ways that help us know how better to address their well-being, engage them in meaningful learning, and give them feedback. As a teacher and professor, that has looked different for me over the years as I have served elementary through doctoral students, but the principles are the same. The following three principles—and their associated warnings—frame my approach to knowing each student. I have also seen these principles demonstrated over and over again in the hundreds of schools I have studied. We need to be curious, make time, and demonstrate love.

Be Genuinely Curious

Warning: People, especially kids, know when your curiosity is not genuine.

Truly curious teachers are more interested in what students are saying than in what they themselves have to say. To help a student thrive, teachers have to build communities of learners who are genuinely interested in the perspectives of others. Wiggins and McTighe (2005) list empathy as the highest form of understanding. Genuine curiosity is essential for empathy and, therefore, for deep understanding.

Genuine curiosity can take multiple forms. In my elementary and middle school teaching days, for example, curiosity looked like eating lunch with students and going to their games, plays, and performances. Seeing students outside of class fed my curiosity and offered avenues within the classroom to build the curiosity of other students. As a teacher, I could genuinely say to the class, "Imani is an amazing ballerina; did you all know that? I saw her perform last night." "Did you know that Gus is an expert on Pluto? I learned so much about planets and dwarf planets at lunch yesterday." When we model this as teachers and administrators, we become co-learners driven by curiosity.

Another way to show curiosity is by simply checking in on a student's well-being, particularly when they're absent from class. For instance, when a student misses one of my college classes, I email or text them first to check on their physical and mental health. I also let them know that we missed their perspective in class and that our class was poorer because they were not there. High school English teacher Katie Kilpatrick takes a similar approach:

> When we record class when a student is absent for an extended period of time, we start class by waving at the recording iPad and greeting that student by name. When a student is out sick, we take the first 30 seconds of class to all email or text that student to let them know they're missed.

These simple practices change the dynamic of a classroom.

Demonstrating curiosity about a student nurtures a culture of curiosity in classrooms. We want students to be interested in each other. This curiosity enriches learning and allows each student to be seen and known—especially because this is not entirely contingent on the teacher. In other words, when students complete our classes, we do not want them to miss the teacher as much as we want them to miss our class and the curiosity-driven community we have developed.

> When students complete our classes, we do not want them to miss the teacher as much as we want them to miss our class and the curiosity-driven community we have developed.

One practice has transformed my teaching because of the curiosity it demonstrates and fosters. While I use this with graduate and undergraduate students, I have seen this stoke curiosity in kindergarten classrooms, too. In fact, many of the most effective teaching practices I use with adults I see demonstrated in kindergarten classrooms. The practice is a formalized version of Doug Lemov's "show call" that involves taking students' written work and displaying it to the class (Lemov, 2021). In my version, I require students to submit their learning responses on our learning management system (LMS) by 10:00 PM the night before class. This gives me time before class to read each response and structure class around the different perspectives each student brings to class. For K–12 teachers, the corollary would be to quickly review exit tickets and highlight some questions or learning the next day (see Box 1.1). This practice of stoking curiosity is beneficial in at least four ways:

1) We give timely feedback to students on our LMS or in class. When I first started teaching, grading would pile up for me. This is not the case when I have only a few hours before teaching the class.

2) Students' responses take us out of our own heads and into theirs. Their insights can be powerful and often improve our teaching.

3) We pull quotes from various students' responses and embed them in learning experiences in each class. When the slide appears, the student who has written the response immediately reads it to the class, and we discuss the perspective. In K–12 classrooms, having students explain their own work makes them the teacher.

4) The fact that students know that their perspectives will shape class and that anything they write could be elevated in this way significantly increases the effort they put into reading and writing, which enhances the quality of their thinking.

1.1 Just Teaching Strategy

Stoking Curiosity

1) Identify good thinking in a student work sample or exit slip.

2) Integrate two to three examples of student work into the following day's lesson.

3) On a document camera or digital image capture of their work, display the students' work at an appropriate point in the following day's lesson.

4) Make the students teachers. Ask students to explain their thinking.

As educators, one of our jobs is to elicit our students' stories. Building class around their responses is a form of eliciting their stories. Emdin (2016) takes this practice to a higher art form. He invites barbers into his college classroom to help teachers understand how to get students to share who they are. Emdin contends that barbers are successful because they are effective at eliciting the stories of their customers (in addition to being good at cutting hair, of course). Master barber Marcus Harvey says, "Clients walk into my shop to get a haircut, but as a master of my craft, my responsibility is to ensure that the client leaves the barbershop having had a personal experience with me that makes them want to come back. It's bigger than just a haircut" (p. 57). Good educators, like good barbers, use stories and humor to break through negativity or anxiety. They understand the broader culture around a student. Emdin includes a key insight from Marcus Harvey, who said that "cutting a white dude's hair is different than cutting a black dude's hair. I had to take time out to learn how to cut white hair. I needed to get new tools to give haircuts to people who weren't black because the texture of their hair was different. I really had to practice a new approach" (p. 58). These insights are essential for us as educators as we seek new tools and approaches to give each student a personal experience.

Asking questions, listening, and telling brief stories about ourselves with appropriate levels of self-disclosure go a long way toward creating the types of classroom environments that breed curiosity and elicit stories. One of the most effective tools I use in professional learning conferences and have seen used in K–12 classrooms is to lead with a story of failure or struggle. The purpose of sharing these stories is to show how we can learn and grow together through vulnerability. We can then ask students to identify how willing they are to learn from failure or struggle and ask them to distribute themselves on a human continuum in the room from "least likely to learn from failure" to "most likely to learn from failure." Students then have two minutes each to share with a partner near them on the continuum an example of how they have taken a risk, failed, and learned. Then we ask for a few volunteers to share with the whole group. This builds curiosity, creates connections between participants, connects me to them, and allows each person to be heard by at least one other person (see Box 1.2).

1.2 Just Teaching Strategy

Elevate Struggle

1) Lead by example: Share a story of your own struggle or failure. This does not have to end in success, merely in learning that demonstrates your own growth through vulnerability.

2) On the wall or on a screen, designate one end of the room as "least likely to learn from failure" and the other as "most likely to learn from failure."

3) Have students move to where they think they fall on the continuum.

4) Give students two minutes each to share a story of their own struggle or failure with the only requirement being that they had to learn something from the struggle/failure.

5) Ask for two to three volunteers to share their stories and what they learned.

6) Celebrate the vulnerability, learning, and story of growth.

Make Time, Especially When It Is Not Convenient

Warning: Student needs are not contingent on your schedule. If you miss your window, you might not get another opportunity.

We have to build time into our schedules for the unpredictable needs of students. As educators, we can very easily become victims of the tyranny of the urgent. There will always be papers to grade, bureaucratic requirements, parents to contact, and lessons to plan. However, we cannot lose sight of the very best part of teaching: our students. When I get to the end of my career, I am not going to look back on a well-crafted rubric, amazing professional learning community protocol, email, lesson plan, or even this book as my raison d'être. Individual students are the reason for my existence. I see students as immortal beings who have immeasurable value. How I treat them each day matters far more than what I accomplish or what institution I serve. My willingness to stop and listen might be the most important thing I do each day.

> My willingness to stop and listen might be the most important thing I do each day.

This means that I am always ready to talk before or after class and that I welcome meals with students whenever we can make them work. With college students, this means I am also inviting students into my home to discuss books and movies or to join family game nights. This is my favorite part of being a professor. My work is so much richer because of the time outside of class with students. An ancillary benefit is that this time investment pays significant dividends in class because attendance improves, I understand content more completely, and students are more likely to learn because I am building on their prior knowledge and experiences.

Seeking students out in the hall, at lunch, before school, after school, coaching, or sponsoring a club are all great ways to show them that you value them as individuals beyond the classroom. As a classroom teacher, it was always important for me to spend time with students that they knew I did not have to spend with them. I was a middle school basketball and tennis coach for girls and boys. Sometimes I needed reminders of why I was doing this. If you have coached middle school athletes, you probably understand. One particularly low moment was when my very talented group of soccer players (who also played basketball for a couple of months a year) lost a basketball game 32–6. I called my brother (who was a college basketball coach) to ask him why I was coaching middle school basketball. He reminded me, "Coaching middle school sports is not about winning. You are doing this to build relationships." Of course, he was right; this reframed the rest of the season as his words—a simple echo of what I had told him in the past about my *why*—were exactly what I needed to hear.

In *The Novice Advantage* (Eckert, 2016b), I highlighted the 2x10 strategy (Smith & Lambert, 2008). In one study, disruptive classroom behaviors decreased by 85% for students who were the focus of the strategy (see Box 1.3). I have employed this strategy from elementary to graduate school, and it works—especially when time is limited. For two minutes a day for ten days, I engage a student who is particularly challenging in a conversation about anything. While this can be awkward at first, simply by seeking the student out and engaging with them, I begin to learn more about this student. Engagement increases because the student begins to feel seen and known, while I am simultaneously seeing and knowing in deeper ways.

1.3 Just Teaching Strategy

2x10

1) For two minutes a day for ten days, talk to one student who has been challenging to get to know. Beware: The first few days will probably be tough, so do some good observation. Who does the student hang out with? What do they show interest in? What do they wear? Do they have any siblings? Another hack is to have students give you some basic information about themselves through a survey. I had an "11 Weird Things About Me" survey that came complete with "Would you eat beef liver cat food, pork rinds, and strawberry Yoo-hoo for $50?" My older brother actually consumed all these items for free—long story. While these questions seem random, they are an opening for a conversation.

2) Based on your observations or survey, find two to three things that you are genuinely curious about and formulate at least three questions. You might burn through all three the first day! Here are some optional starter questions, but remember: The more you can tailor the question to the student, the better:

   "When you are not in class, what do you like to do?"

   "Would you eat the strawberry Yoo-hoo, pork rinds, and beef liver cat food for $50?"

   "What is one thing that would make our class better?" (Don't get defensive!)

3) Keep a small journal or digital file to help you keep track of who you're meeting with and when.

4) Use what you know about the student to help individualize instruction and be responsive to their interests, talents, and needs.

In the United States, suicide is the second leading cause of death among 14- to 18-year-olds. In 2019, 18.8% of students reported having seriously considered suicide (Ivey-Stephenson et al., 2020). Now that I have taught long enough to have attended funerals of students, I am increasingly convinced that each minute I have spent seeing and knowing students has been the most valuable time I have spent. Burying a student is almost as unnatural as a parent burying a child. However, it provides perspective. While I hope this is not the case for you, if you have had a student take their own life, this changes you. It changed me as a teacher. We need to take the time to listen when students are ready to share. We might be the only lifeline they reach for. Not to be grandiose, but we might be the connection they need to get the help that will save them. As we build community in our schools and classrooms, we cannot be the only ones doing this work because this will overwhelm us. Every adult and student in the building needs to be looking out for others and finding the people who need a 2x10. If we have 2,500 educators, staff, and students in a high school looking out for each other, school culture will improve and we are all more likely to thrive.

Demonstrate Love to Cultivate Joy

Warning: Our joy diminishes in direct proportion to our lack of love for each student.

As teachers and administrators, we are only as strong as our weakest students. Our joy comes from seeing students grow. Our desire to see them grow flows from our love for them as individuals. Some students are hard to love. In one of my all-time favorite TED talks, Rita Pierson speaks inspirational truth to educators and emphasizes that every kid needs a champion. I am inspired by almost all of what she says. However, I disagree with one point that she makes toward the end of her talk. Pierson says,

> Will you always like all your children? Of course not. And you know your toughest kids are never absent. You won't like them all, and the tough ones show up for a reason. It is the connection. It is the relationship. And while you won't like them all, the key is they can never ever know it. That is why teachers become great actors and great actresses.

I have struggled to like some students, but I would caution against becoming an actor. Students see through acting. The toughest students for me to like have always been wealthy, entitled students who communicate "You are *just* a teacher" with one look. They can make me feel small and inconsequential. However, 26 years into teaching, I can honestly say that I have not had to be an actor and pretend to like them. The way forward for me was to demonstrate love for each of those students even when I did not feel that love. To do that, I would sit in the student's seat in the early morning before school would start and pray for them and their well-being. Sitting in the seat and trying to understand where the student was coming from altered my perspective. I would force myself to find something good in that student every day and point it out or write it down somewhere so that I could express gratitude. Over time, as I cultivated the practice of demonstrating love for that student, my attitude would change in a way that would not allow the student to steal my joy. My actions precipitated a change in my feelings (see Box 1.4). As my feelings toward the students changed, my joy increased. In some cases, the students who had originally been the most difficult for me to love became some of the markers of professional joy as I saw them begin to thrive.

1.4 Just Teaching Strategy

Demonstrate Love to Cultivate Joy

1) Identify a student you are struggling to love.

2) Sit in their seat before school and look at the classroom from their perspective.

3) Identify at least one good quality about the student while sitting in their seat.

4) Write the quality down in a private notebook or audio record the quality in a private digital file and return to it as frequently as needed until you are grateful for the student and working for their well-being.

5) At an appropriate time, share anything positive you have noticed with the student. Not only will this encourage the student, but this affirmation will also help cement these feelings for you as well.

The tool at the end of the chapter can also support you in this strategy.

Loving each student means we do not have to become actors. We can actively demonstrate love to each student in ways that feed the deep joy that comes from seeing others flourish (Brooks, 2019). This is good for students but even better for us! Putting on a mask or persona and pretending to be something that we are not is suffocating. Sociologist Brené Brown explains why this is not a good idea: "The word *persona* is the Greek term for 'stage mask.' In my work, masks and armor are perfect metaphors for how we protect ourselves from the discomfort of vulnerability. Masks make us feel safer even when they become suffocating" (Brown, 2012, p. 113).

Acting suffocates and steals joy. Finding ways to demonstrate love enhances how we feel about students and allows us to find joy. A precondition for meeting the needs of each student is our joy as teachers. While it is not sufficient to ensure that all students are learning, our joy is necessary. How do we tap curiosity, develop intellectual virtues, or expect our students to find joy in learning if we do not find it there ourselves?

> A precondition for meeting the needs of each student is our joy as teachers.

All of Us for Each of Us

We started the chapter with the statement that we cannot "miss the tree for the forest." We have to see each student. We have to see Anthony. That could be overwhelming and exhausting. However, what if the answer is in the forest?

A few years ago, I visited a sequoia redwood forest in California. That forest was one of the most awe-inspiring testaments to life I have ever experienced. The trees are over 2,500 years old, can grow more than 300 feet high, and can weigh over 6,000 tons. Supporting that kind of life should require deep roots, right?

Wrong. Sequoia redwoods' roots are only 6–12 feet below the soil. How is this possible? Sequoia redwoods function as a community. Each tree is dependent on the other trees as their roots are intertwined. Through these dense networks of roots, they share support and nutrients. Because of their root systems, sequoia redwoods can withstand wind, fire, earthquakes, and storms. They have been doing all that effectively since before our calendar started counting forward!

Our schools and classrooms should function like redwood forests. No individual teacher or administrator can meet all the needs of each student. However, we can create the conditions in which each student can flourish by creating systems of intertwining roots. While we cannot control everything that enhances or diminishes each student's ecosystem (e.g., poverty, family, culture, social media, etc.), we can build communities that support each student. The remainder of this book describes the nutrients and rootedness that we need to grow giants—not individual giants but forests of giants who are interdependent and thrive most when they thrive together. Home, character, academics, and friends are to students as roots, soil, water, nutrients, and sun are to redwoods. We need to understand what assets our students bring to our schools if we are to care for them effectively by providing feedback, engaging hearts and minds, and tending to their well-being.

This is also true for how we should care for our colleagues because we cannot nourish students if educators are withering. We cannot be myopic and only focus on students. In my experience, I have seen many educators extend far more grace to students than they will to colleagues. This cannot continue.

Home, character, academics, and friends are to students as roots, soil, water, nutrients, and sun are to redwoods. We need to understand what assets our students bring to our schools if we are to care for them effectively by providing feedback, engaging hearts and minds, and tending to their well-being.

This is the work we get to do every day as we develop giants. C. S. Lewis writes, "The task of the modern educator is not to cut down jungles but to irrigate deserts" (Lewis, 2001, pp. 13–14). Feedback, engagement, and well-being are that irrigation. Our power lies in our attention to these three things, and they are enhanced when they occur in community. Students can attend to all three of these areas that are the lifeblood of growth when we give them the tools and support to intertwine their roots. When we build thriving communities of learners, our collective impact can outlive even the redwoods and echo through eternity.

There is no big emotional payoff to Anthony's story; at the end of his fifth-grade year in our classroom, Anthony's family moved again and we lost contact. But for a school year, our lives overlapped, and along with a school social worker, a school psychologist, a principal, a learning specialist, and a class of amazing fifth graders, we helped Anthony become the best version of himself. He made significant progress over the course of the year and was nearly at grade level in reading and math and was demonstrating genuine curiosity in science. When he first arrived, he was reticent to speak or play at recess, but he became a talkative kickballer. Because he was safe, fed, seen, and loved, he learned. Could he have learned more? Could we have done better? Absolutely. But we knew what Anthony needed. We attended to his well-being, engaged his mind, and showed him that he was growing through clear, honest feedback. His peers accepted him as part of our collective forest, and I was convinced that he could do well in middle school.

Redwoods are not meant to be transplanted, and they do not thrive when they are on their own. All we can do is care for those around us as our lives become interdependent in deepening community. I hope that in some way, Anthony carries the influence of our community with him and that he has found a forest where he is now a thriving giant.

To not miss the tree in the forest, we need to be sure the forest is looking out for each tree.

Just Teaching Tool #1
Four Lenses

This first tool is designed to help you look at each student so you can create a forest that grows each student into a thriving giant. Feel free to do this with others, especially if you are in upper grades and share students. You can download a fillable PDF from resources.corwin.com/justteaching

1) Think of the student you are struggling to connect with the most. Write their name in the center box.

2) Look at the student through the four lenses to identify assets that could help your community (your forest) support and feed growth.

3) After including as many assets as possible, identify a next step for each of the four lenses that will allow the student to thrive and take action. What could you do to connect friends, your academic content, their own character development, or their home to your work together?

4) Repeat for as many students as you need to see better. This can be the focus of your 2x10.

Extend yourself grace. You will not get this right the first time. As the experts in improvement science write, "Our work is possibly wrong and definitely incomplete" (Bryk et al., 2015, p. 79). Don't let perfection be the enemy of improvement.

(Continued)

(Continued)

TOOL #1 | **FOUR LENSES**

THE FOREST CAN HELP US SEE EACH TREE, SO WE CAN GROW GIANTS

THINK OF THE STUDENT YOU ARE STRUGGLING TO CONNECT WITH THE MOST

LENS 1

FRIENDS
"SUN"

What assets do the student's friends add? How can we leverage positive peer influence? Extracurricular involvement? What other friends does the student need?

˅

NEXT STEP

LENS 2

ACADEMICS
"NUTRIENTS/WATER"

What assets does the student bring academically? What passions or interests do they have? Where is the greatest potential for growth?

˅

NEXT STEP

LENS 3

character
"SOIL"

What character traits are assets for this students? What character traits need to develop? What are some vehicles for developing character that might serve the student well?

˅

NEXT STEP

LENS 4

HOME
"ROOTS"

What assets does the student bring from home? Community? Culture? What else do you need to know? How might you deepen your understanding?

˅

NEXT STEP

> " **REMEMBER OUR WORK IS POSSIBLY WRONG AND DEFINITELY INCOMPLETE.** "
>
> BRYK ET AL., 2015, P.79

SCAN THE QR CODE
FOR A FILLABLE PDF

Part I

Well-Being

The next two chapters explore how we can attend to the well-being of our students and ourselves. If we are not well, then engagement and feedback do not matter. Well-being is the foundation and the outcome of teaching because it is all about thriving educators serving thriving students.

FEEDBACK, ENGAGEMENT, & **WELL-BEING**

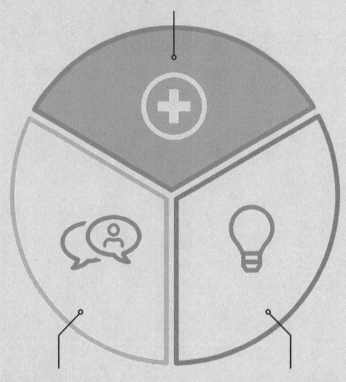

WELL-BEING
PURPOSE-DRIVEN FLOURISHING

FEEDBACK
PURPOSE-DRIVEN
WISDOM FOR GROWTH

ENGAGEMENT
CONTENT, CONSOLIDATION,
COLLABORATION, CREATION

Maslow Before Bloom

2

We have to Maslow before we Bloom.

Joel Gaines

Just Teaching

Chapter 2 "Decomplexified"

- Purpose-driven flourishing is the goal of education and is for the common good.

- Attending to well-being is not additional work; instead, it is the way we do our work.

- We need less cortisol and more serotonin, dopamine, and oxytocin.
  - To increase these without creating more work, we need to
    - augh,
    - play,
    - elicit stories,
    - model gratitude,
    - create moments,
    - have fun,
    - see whole people, and
    - develop empathic capacity.

Hope

Hope Academy is located in Minneapolis, Minnesota, on Chicago Avenue, 14 blocks from the site where a police officer placed his knee on the neck of George Floyd, a handcuffed Black man, until he stopped breathing while bystanders yelled at the officer to stop. Makeshift memorials of pictures, flowers, street art, and larger-than-life Brown fists thrust into the air occupy street intersections. Concrete barriers, fences, razor wire, and boarded-up windows surround the police precinct that no longer functions. More than a year removed from the murder, pain is still palpable.

But there is hope—both literally and figuratively. The neighborhood that surrounds Hope Academy is home to people of many ethnicities who speak over 100 languages. The city park next to the school has been renovated recently, and there are restaurants that provide tastes of far-flung international cuisine. Founded in 2000, the school moved into its current location, a converted hospital, in 2006 and serves students in kindergarten through Grade 12.

Grades 6–12 are divided into Houses—think Hogwarts and Hufflepuff, Ravenclaw, and Gryffindor with nothing as evil as Slytherin—and compete for points through academic and other culture-building friendly competitions. I happened to visit the school on a House Feast Day where students brought in different kinds of foods from their own backgrounds. I observed a joyful, peaceful school community (other than a few complaints about the cold outdoor setting for the feast).

Hope Academy has prioritized Maslow's hierarchy of needs. Abraham Maslow (1954) described human physiological, safety, and belonging needs as foundational to cognitive needs. Benjamin Bloom et al. (1956) identified six levels of educational learning objectives: knowledge, comprehension, application, analysis, synthesis, and evaluation. Any U.S. educator over the past 60 years has likely been influenced by both Maslow's and Bloom's work. Good schools do not prioritize Bloom over Maslow. As Joel Gaines, a head of school from Philadelphia, often says, "We Maslow before we Bloom." Certainly, Hope Academy is not alone in the way it addresses physiological, safety, belonging, and esteem needs in support of cognitive needs because we know that effective educators attend to Maslow in the service of Bloom.

Similar to other effective educators, Hope Academy's teachers are trained in trauma-informed, culturally responsive teaching practices. We know more now about how the brain works and how to engage minds than at any point in human history. The key to learning is applying that knowledge so that we all—educators, students, and communities—can flourish.

What We Know: Purpose-Driven Flourishing

The landscape around social-emotional learning can be confusing and overwhelming, with so much being written about social-emotional learning, noncognitive factors, character, and civic, equitable, just, moral, and purposeful education (e.g., The Collaborative for Academic, Social, and Emotional Learning [CASEL]; Marvin Berkowitz's PRIMED; Angela Duckworth's Character Lab; the University of Birmingham's Jubilee Centre). However, the terms get close to the heart of why we went into education in the first place. What we do as educators is about so much more than phonemes, periodic tables, politics, Pythagoras, and punctuation—we are far more interested in developing people.

Whatever term we use, we know that Maslow's hierarchy of needs is grounded in what we have in common as human beings. In this book, we will use the term *well-being*. For our purposes, well-being represents "purpose-driven flourishing." Going back to Aristotle, this is the true purpose of education as it serves the individual and public good. Purpose-driven flourishing is learning for the common good. By taking this timeless approach, we can move past some of the politics and confusion of the "educationese" that seem to swirl all around us.

Parents want purpose-driven flourishing for their children. In a recent survey, parents were asked to rank phrases associated with social and emotional learning. The phrase *social-emotional learning* (SEL) was extremely unpopular. Parents also did not like phrases such as *soft skills* or *growth mindset* because they felt like they were not focused on academic content and were a form of indoctrination. Does this mean that parents do not value this kind of learning? When the researchers added the word *academic* to make the phrase *social-emotional and academic learning*, parents rated this as the second most important focus of schools. They also reported broad support for all nine SEL-related skills on the survey (see Figure 2.1).

By focusing on the three elements of just teaching, schools thrive as educators and students develop character and enact virtues. Focus on the well-being wedge of our model in Figure 2.2. If educators and students are able to pursue purpose-driven flourishing because they are mentally, emotionally, and physically well, then they will create schools built on love and justice because those schools will be filled with leaders—both

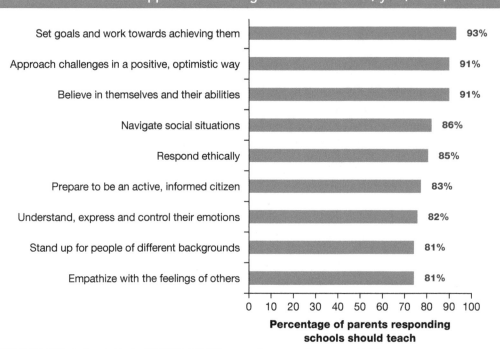

FIGURE 2.1   Parental Support for Teaching SEL-Related Skills (Tyner, 2021)

educators and students—who have the capacity and desire to enact moral virtues such as compassion, courage, gratitude, honesty, humility, integrity, justice, and respect. We will discuss the feedback and engagement wedges in subsequent chapters, but when we enact just teaching practices, those practices ripple out in virtuous concentric circles that enhance teaching and learning. This is not another character program or a moralistic paradigm. As Parker Palmer writes, "Good teaching cannot be reduced to technique; good teaching comes from the identity and integrity of the teacher" (1998, p. 10). This model is not a program or even a process; this is how and why we teach.

Moving from the philosophical to the practical, we have to create conditions in which students can thrive. Constant turbulence in the learning environment impedes flourishing (Urick et al., 2021). Mark Brackett, director of the Center for Emotional Intelligence at Yale University, said, "If you don't know how to deal with the lack of control of your future or the feeling of uncertainty that you're having, your brain is going to stay in a constant fight or flight mode. And if your brain is in flight or fight mode, then it is not in learning mode" (Prothero, 2020). Given all the challenges students are facing from disrupted learning, school shootings, toxic social media, or adverse childhood experiences (ACEs), students are likely to be in a heightened state of flight or fight.

FIGURE 2.2   Just Teaching for School and Personal Character

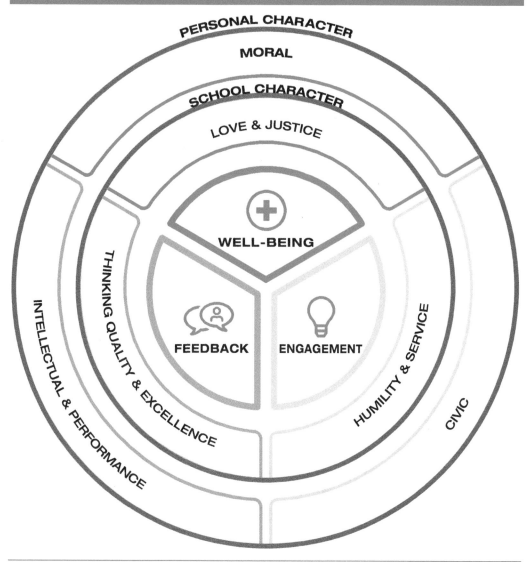

At Yale's Center for Emotional Intelligence (CEI), Marc Brackett and his colleagues use an approach called RULER, an acronym for the five skills of emotional intelligence: recognizing, understanding, labeling, expressing, and regulating emotions. The CEI focuses on teaching these skills to teachers and administrators in the building so that they can become more emotionally intelligent in their work with students. As their emotional intelligence increases, the school climate improves, which is

(Continued)

(Continued)

essential for students who have experienced numerous adverse childhood experiences (Pawlo et al., 2019). This approach is based on evidence that emotions affect attention, memory, and learning. Additionally, emotions affect our decision-making, influence our social relationships, drive our health, and influence our creativity and effectiveness (Heller, 2017).

There are numerous strategies that can help students manage emotions and stress. While none of these are panaceas, they might provide some inspiration.

- Create a calm environment by focusing on ways to relax, focusing on positive behaviors, using therapy dogs, and playing classical music.

- Ensure safety by being explicit about innate human dignity and de-escalation (e.g., instead of telling a student "Pick that up," say "Pick that up before lunchtime" to allow the student to think rationally and not create a power struggle [Minahan, 2019]), journaling, and creating space for individual work and reflection.

- Building on RULER, give students the opportunity to articulate their feelings through check-ins that are developmentally appropriate (Spiegel, 2017).

While there are multiple tools and trainings available, the sheer number of trainings and what is required can sometimes add to our sense of feeling overwhelmed. The most important step is to be more aware of our emotions and the emotions of others. This awareness takes very little additional time, energy, or resources, and we can make significant progress.

Books on the neuroscience of learning have proliferated over the last few decades (Bransford et al., 2000; Hammond, 2015; Hattie & Yates, 2014; McTighe & Willis, 2019; National Academies of Sciences, Engineering & Medicine, 2018; Sousa & Tomlinson, 2011). For our purposes, we are not going to delve deeply into the anatomy and physiology of the brain, but we are going to take a few key concepts from medical and education research and apply them to our schools. For more in-depth but accessible reading, see any of the authors cited above.

We need to be careful not to use reductionistic thinking when we consider the neuroscience behind everything that goes on in classroom interactions. We are learning more and more about our brains and their chemistry, but we would be just as mistaken if we reduced human interactions to chemicals as policymakers are when they consider children to be test scores. However, a basic understanding of what happens in the brain when we are confronted with challenges, opportunities, success, failure, and risk is important for us as professionals.

The Brain's Responses

Zaretta Hammond (2015) describes the way our brain's "safety–threat system" works (p. 45). We need to understand this in order to keep the amygdala from hijacking a student's response. If the amygdala senses danger, it presents the student with four options: flight, fight, freeze, or appease.

- When we see *flight*, we see students who have completely disengaged physically, mentally, or both.

- We see students *fight* when they actively resist what they are being told to do. In other words, it's the reaction we usually get when teachers try to force-feed learning.

- We see students *freezing* when their bodies are present but they lack the ability to respond because they are overwhelmed by the challenge or risk.

- We see students *appease* the teacher, coach, or administrator when they do whatever they are asked to do but without any personal investment. While these instincts might help students survive, none of these options are good for significant, deeper learning.

We want to move students from avoiding to approaching to attaching. There are significant chemical rewards from the brain to individuals when we move from left to right in Figure 2.3. When we sense a threat, the sympathetic nervous system kicks in to protect us through the activation of the reticular activating system (RAS) and the amygdala. For example, if they see someone humiliated or injured due to bullying in the classroom, students are going to fight, flee, freeze, or appease. The brain releases cortisol, which is the hormone that the brain releases when it is in distress. When this happens, they are not in a frame of mind to learn.

FIGURE 2.3   The Brain's Safety–Threat System

SYSTEMS	AVOIDING	APPROACHING	ATTACHING
PURPOSE	Detect threats to physical, social, and psychological threats	Seek out well-being and reward despite obstacles	Connect with others in order to increase protection and connection
BRAIN STRUCTURES	Reticular Activating System (RAS), Amygdala, Sympathetic Nervous System	RAS, Thalamus, Neocortex, Parasympathetic Nervous System	RAS & Polyvagal Nervous System
SELECT HORMONES	Cortisol	Dopamine & Serotonin	Oxytocin

Adapted from Zaretta Hammond, *Culturally Responsive Teaching and The Brain*. Corwin Press, 2015, p. 45.

We have all seen the consequences of students feeling threatened in a school situation. When students enter fight mode, they become defensive or aggressive. They lash out to protect themselves. If they enter flight mode, they disengage or disappear. If they freeze, they are not able to engage with others or meaningfully engage in learning. If they enter appease mode, they become mentally absent or only go through the motions. While appeasement might seem to be preferable to fight, flight, or freeze, the fact that it might be less obtrusive or even noticeable is problematic. In all four modes—fight, flight, freeze, and appease—the student has disengaged and cortisol is released. Additionally, when the student is only appeasing an authority figure, their lack of real engagement goes unnoticed, with no possibility for growth.

We want less cortisol, and more dopamine, serotonin, and oxytocin. All four are hormones that aid communication between nerve cells. Dopamine rewards us for focusing our attention and finding interesting things. Serotonin stabilizes our moods, happiness, and overall sense of well-being. Oxytocin is sometimes referred to as the "bonding hormone" because it is typically released when relational trust is present. We want learning environments with appropriate levels of challenge for each student and connections between learners so that each student can approach learning and attach to others.

Cultivating environments that reduce cortisol production and increase dopamine, serotonin, and oxytocin production will enhance learning in the short term and, over time, significantly benefit the human body. In the best-selling book, *The Body Keeps the Score* (2014), medical doctor Bessel Van Der Kolk highlights the way our responses to trauma and positive connections affect our minds and bodies. He cites research that one in five Americans has been molested, one in four has grown up with alcoholics, and one in three couples has engaged in physical violence. That is a lot of cortisol for a lot of students. Over time, trauma like this leads to a loss of physical health through increased risk for diabetes, heart disease, obesity, and high blood pressure. Mentally, people are at greater risk of loneliness, depression, and suicide. However, as educators, if we can create conditions in which students can connect with others and approach new challenges, they can thrive, setting themselves up for future success as their brains and bodies are wired for health.

What Works in Real Schools: More Dopamine, Serotonin, and Oxytocin

Here are a few simple ways to create learning environments that produce more dopamine, serotonin, and oxytocin and less cortisol:

Laugh

Laughing and smiling put our brains in a more positive state because they reduce cortisol and release endorphins. Marcia Tate (2016) reminds us that laughter, even fake laughter, has a positive effect on the brain so, as she recommends, just laugh (see Box 2.1). We are also 30 times more likely to laugh when we are with others than when we are alone (Price, 2021), so odds are good that laughter is more likely to occur when we are together in class.

> Cultivating environments that reduce cortisol production and increase dopamine, serotonin, and oxytocin production will enhance learning in the short term and, over time, significantly benefit the human body.

Humor can be a powerful tool in the classroom, but Tate reminds us not to confuse humor with sarcasm. According to the Merriam-Webster dictionary (2010), sarcasm comes from the Greek verb *sarkazein*, which literally means "to tear flesh like a dog." Sarcasm, unlike humor, is likely to demean others in a way that causes students or colleagues to avoid learning opportunities. To be clear, all these techniques are designed to enhance content, knowledge, and skills.

2.1 Just Teaching Strategy

Laugh

Here are a few strategies that might increase healthy laughter.

1. Curate funny videos that relate to your content. Find clips on YouTube, Twitter, Instagram, Facebook, or whatever app you prefer that make you laugh. If appropriate, share them with students and

(Continued)

(Continued)

colleagues. I keep a collection of links I love and use in professional learning sessions here:

2. Look for humor every day. Students say and do entertaining things every day. We devoted one entire whiteboard in our seventh-grade science lab to funny quotes from students that remained up all year. I also have a journal full of outrageous things students have said and done in my classrooms. Every time I read this journal I laugh.

Links to humorous videos and content

3. Take yourself less seriously. If we can keep this perspective, we can certainly find many ways to laugh each day.

Play

Even in the doctoral classes I teach, we play games because doctoral students are not really that different from the middle school students I taught. A good game of Gimkit, Kahoot!, or a simulation will create a high level of engagement among seasoned educational professionals. The key is to create the right kind of friendly competition. Every student needs to be able to engage and be successful and should be competing against themselves for their own improvement. We regularly conduct simulations that allow every student to play a well-researched role, with the remainder of the students serving as active feedback providers for their peers. When done well, play engages the brain in meaningful ways that can stimulate learning while establishing trust (see Box 2.2).

2.2 Just Teaching Strategy

Play

Here are a few ideas to consider when thinking about how to play games more effectively (this is an abbreviated and updated list from Eckert, 2016b).

1. **Every student needs a reason to listen to and answer every question every time.** Whether we are using smart devices or pulling popsicle sticks out of a can, every student needs to listen to every question, which means that each student has to be able to buzz in or have the opportunity to be called on to answer.

2. **You and your students should all enjoy playing the game.** If you do not, find a new game.

3. **Cooperative games are effective for keeping students engaged.** If students are competing against one another and they realize that they cannot win, they will defensively shut down. Give them a reason to collaborate and help each other be successful. Winning does not necessarily mean there have to be losers. Getting everyone over the finish line should be our goal. Make sure students are primarily competing for their own improvement so that there is always a reason to compete.

4. **Even if students are playing in teams, be sure that everyone has to answer at some point.** After a question is asked in a game, make sure there is time for individuals and teams to process the answer. The great thing about games such as Gimkit is that every student has to answer every question. If you are playing a live game in class, give students time to discuss as a team and then rotate the spokesperson so that everyone is responsible, even if not everyone can answer every question directly.

Elicit Stories

As I highlighted in Chapter 1 through the example of barbers, great teachers elicit and disclose stories. Our brains are wired for stories. Even before humans could write things down, we have communicated through stories and we can approach difficult concepts through stories. From Holocaust novels for intermediate students to case studies for graduate students, a well-told story draws others into learning and builds empathic capacity (see Box 2.3).

 2.3 Just Teaching Strategy

Elicit Stories

1. Identify one or two of your own stories that have been effective for you in connecting with students. Typically, these are stories of our own failures in which we have learned something. Remember, sometimes our weaknesses are our strengths for connecting

(Continued)

(Continued)

with others. For me, my stories of struggling as a kindergartener with dyslexia, a high school student in West Virginia, or my 2–20 basketball season—we beat the same team twice—as a senior are often good entry points.

2. Refine the story into a two- to three-minute compelling version. Share it.

3. Create space for students to share their stories. This can be before class, after class, at lunch, or as a follow-up to your story. Choose your story-sharing times wisely: Kindergarten teachers know that student storytelling can spiral out of control into 5-year-old one-upmanship. Those of us who teach middle school and beyond have to be intentional about creating this space as students are far more reticent.

4. Look for unique things in each student that others might overlook. Ask questions that give you insights into students' stories.

Model Gratitude

Researchers have found that positive emotional states improve learning and memory and that gratitude specifically motivates people to engage in self-improvement (Armenta et al., 2017). Greg McKeown (2021) reminds us of the benefit of gratitude: "When you focus on what you lack, you lose what you have. When you focus on what you have, you get what you lack" (pp. 58–59). Personally, I have found gratitude to be remarkably beneficial to my own emotional state and learning. Social media in general, and Twitter specifically, is not typically a venue people think of when they consider gratitude (see Box 2.4). We are more likely to associate social media with vitriol, fear of missing out, or the polished and filtered lives of others that we only wish we had. However, one year when I was feeling particularly cut off from others due to a move to a new state and an isolating pandemic, I decided to use Twitter differently. My bio on Twitter has been "grateful teacher and learner" for years, but each day between March 18, 2020–March 18, 2021, I posted something for which I was grateful. Some days this was easy, but on other days, I really had to dig. The habit changed the way I thought about life and freed me to engage other people.

Jasmine Bayliss, a school leader outside of Dallas, lives out her gratitude related to education:

> I've always felt grateful for the opportunity to be in school because my parents did not have that opportunity. My dad dropped out of school when he was 12 to care for his mom and sister. When the Communists took over North Vietnam, they sent his father to a work reeducation camp. My grandfather never returned home. My mom stopped attending school at 15 because her father could not afford to send her to school beyond that. I grew up with the belief that being educated was a blessing and an opportunity that not everyone gets.

Jasmine took that gratitude all the way to Harvard University, where she completed her undergraduate degree.

2.4 Just Teaching Strategy

Positive Venting

Do you find venting to be helpful? For years, I believed that venting was healthy, and perhaps some forms of it are. Certainly, there have been plenty of very hard things to process through these past few years. However, when I vent, I have to ask myself a few questions (Eckert, 2016b):

- What am I venting about?
- Who am I venting to?
- Did I seek this person out because they will agree with me and confirm my anger and frustration?
- Is this person likely to challenge my perspective or help me reframe the situation in a solution-oriented way?

I know that most of the time when I vent, I feel better because I know I have an ally in my ungratefulness for another person. Ultimately, that brings down two other people and solidifies my negativity.

What about this as an alternative? Let's call it *positive venting*.

- Daily find someone in your life for whom you are grateful.
- Share what you are specifically grateful for about that person with someone else. You do not even necessarily have to let the person for whom you are grateful know. Perhaps it will trickle back to them.
- Do this for one week and see how this changes you and the people around you.

(Continued)

> (Continued)
>
> Need another option? Change your complaining habit (McKeown, 2021).
>
> * Every time you find yourself complaining about something, express one thing for which you are grateful immediately after. In *Effortless*, McKeown means the very next sentence. For example, "My class is driving me crazy today. But I am grateful I get to do meaningful work every day with people who can grow." This is the way to "effortlessly" change the complaining habit.
>
> * For the first few days, you might struggle with this practice, but soon you will find that you will head off your complaint before it is out of your mouth. You might actually become more of an encourager.
>
> When I have tried this, I have found that I begin to look at the world differently and that others begin to do the same.

Create Moments

In their best-selling book, *The Power of Moments,* Chip and Dan Heath (2017) describe how to elevate moments—particularly peaks and ends. We create moments when we elevate events that elicit pride, insight, and/or connection. We cannot do this with every lesson, but we need to do this over the course of a year (see Box 2.5). Heath and Heath describe schools' signing days as an example, where students sign with the colleges they plan to attend in front of every student from sixth grade up.

Teachers can create these moments in their classrooms as well. Brad Thornton, a Chicago-area high school administrator, described the moment an English language arts and physics teacher created a memorable learning experience at his school.

> Their eyes sparkled as they shared the idea, though, and the challenges to pulling it off were quickly consumed by their energy. For six weeks, students were immersed in a project that mirrored the creative process of Disney's Pixar animation studio. Starting with a story idea in English class, students dreamed of characters, conflict, and conclusion. They learned about the Pixar creative process on a field trip to visit a special Pixar exhibit at the Museum of Science and Industry. They built out their story idea using storyboard techniques, pitching ideas to classmates, and getting feedback on how

to sharpen their ideas. Once their character was developed, students brought it to life in physics class, learning the coding and programming necessary to design a visual representation of their character. Students used 3D printers, the laser cutting machine, and other engineering skills informed by physics design principles to build their characters. The project culminated with a presentation in English class that introduced the class to the character and story. On the day of presentations, students walked into school dressed to impress, envisioning their audience as Pixar's creative team looking for the next best story. Student engagement with the project was as enthusiastic as I have seen in high school.

2.5 Just Teaching Strategy

Create Moments

1. Start with your school year as a teacher or administrator. What are the moments in which pride, insight, and/or connection occur for students that you and your school elevate? List them here:

2. Look at each month of the school year. What would be one peak each month that you facilitate for students?

3. Look at each week. What might be a high point of that week for students?

We do not have to make everything into a peak because then we would have created a plateau. However, we do need to elevate certain parts of the year so that there are peaks. We need to pay special attention to what occurs at the end. We want students to end on a peak because that is what they are most likely to remember. Psychologists call this the peak-end rule (Heath & Heath, 2017). How can you and your school end with a peak? How can you create a range of peaks throughout the school year? How can you elevate your school year into the Himalayas instead of the Illinois prairie?

One final note: Do not do all of this thinking on your own. This is a great opportunity to bring in colleagues and students to find opportunities for creating co-owned peaks through tectonic conversations.

Bottom Line: Have Fun

I once started an article with the sentence: "I teach to entertain myself" (Eckert, 2016a). This seemingly self-serving statement was meant to grab readers' attention. However, researchers have confirmed that this is not a bad approach (McTighe & Willis, 2019). In her book, *The Power of Fun: How to Feel Alive Again* (2021), Catherine Price defines *true fun* as "the confluence of playfulness, connection, and flow" (p. 32). She describes *playfulness* as "a spirit of lightheartedness and freedom" (p. 32), *connection* as "the feeling of having a special shared experience with someone (or something) else" (p. 33), and *flow* occurs "when you are fully engrossed and engaged in your present experience to the point that you lose track of the passage of time" (p. 33). When these three overlap (see Figure 2.4), we have what she calls "true fun" which is different than the "fake fun" we might find in something like binge-watching a show. I have certainly experienced this kind of true fun in the classroom. If you have experienced this kind of fun, you know that this is what makes teaching the greatest profession ever.

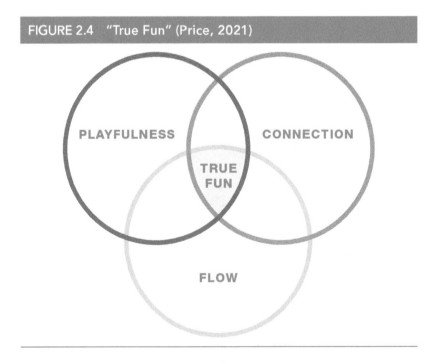

FIGURE 2.4   "True Fun" (Price, 2021)

Our enjoyment of teaching and learning is a precondition for the type of learning environment we want to create for students but is not sufficient to ensure high levels of engagement. We have all sat through high school and college lectures in which the person in the front of the room clearly enjoys hearing themselves talk even while students' enjoyment wanes.

However, if we are not enjoying the learning tasks and experiences we are creating for students, how can we expect them to approach them in a positive way? We are the professionals in the room. If we are not enjoying the experience, it is up to us to change the conditions. We are not here to entertain students, but we certainly can and should have fun with our students. One final clarification: I do not mean turning on a movie and popping some popcorn. We need to make meaningful learning the reward. As educators, we should certainly be able to model that if we are well (see Box 2.6).

2.6 Just Teaching Strategy

Playfulness + Connection + Flow = True Fun

- Identify when you are playful in the classroom. How can you build more of that into each day?

- Identify when you feel the most connected to your students. How can you create more of those connections each day?

- When have you experienced flow in your teaching? More importantly, when have your students experienced flow in their learning? How can you create more opportunities for flow in your classroom?

Reminder, even if you cannot achieve all three at the same time, playfulness, connection, and flow all lead to positive emotions for those involved. Shoot for the moon. If your class only gets out of the Earth's atmosphere, remember that people pay Elon Musk a lot of money for that experience! Don't let perfection be the enemy of fun.

See Whole People

The conditions that educators cultivate for learning have to flow from their own well-being. In one study of over 3,000 students and 1,000 teachers, researchers found that higher teacher well-being is linked to higher student well-being. While this might seem obvious, the research confirmed the importance of teacher–student relationships and that teachers who are not attending to their own well-being might not be capable of developing strong relationships with students. Students who have stronger relationships with teachers have a stronger sense of belonging and connectedness at their schools (Harding et al., 2019). So how do we build those connections?

Sometimes, building connection only requires a brief conversation for a person to be seen and known. One of our primary responsibilities as educators is to connect with each student. Here are two examples that demonstrate how listening and connecting with students transform our ability to educate. The first is from Cierra Nickerson, a Houston-area principal, and the second is from Kyle Taylor, an assistant principal in a rural Texas school. (The student names in both examples are pseudonyms.) While both are administrators, there are lessons for clear takeaways for teachers as well. Principal Cierra Nickerson shared the following:

> I had been principal for two days at my alternative high school for students who are under credited and over age. Each one of them has a different story and a set of circumstances that bring them to our school. Many of our students have been left behind from their traditional high school, unattended, or unchecked. Many of them have slipped through the cracks and face embarrassment and low self-esteem. Some of them engage in unhealthy coping mechanisms. It is vitally important to meet each student where they are on their journey in order for them to be successful and meet their goals.
>
> One student, Monique, arrived on one of our late buses this particular morning. She was known for being rude, snappy, and ready to pop off. As I greeted her, I noticed that she had her hair styled in a very cute way. It was so creative and even used different colored rubber bands. I immediately thought of my own daughter. I led with that. "Your hair is so cute!" I said to her. "Who did it?"
>
> "I did, Miss." She then pulled out her phone and further explained, "I do hair." At that moment, I was completely in awe. On her Instagram, she revealed many photos of her finished products. They were absolutely beautiful. Selfishly, I'm now thinking about myself and allowing Monique to do my hair! She was so proud to show me all the different styles and different clients that she had. I then asked her for her business card (which she didn't have). The AP [assistant principal] and I discussed in front of her how much more profitable her business could be once she made some cards and created a business plan. She thanked us for our ideas with a huge smile on her face and went on to class. The AP then told me that Monique *never* smiled and that she barely

spoke to anyone. The only time they heard her was when she was arguing or telling someone off.

I now plan to bring in a few Houston hair braiders to come and chat with some of our ladies who are into beauty and hair and nails. I would like the community mentors to share with the girls their experiences, journey, and pitfalls. Whenever I learn about the gifts and talents of my students, I plan to provide them access to models and mentors around the community to reinforce their dreams.

Cierra saw Monique as a human being with creative talent. With a simple, insightful compliment and question, she initiated a connection that led to a rare smile and a plan to help more students be seen, known, and elevated.

Assistant principal Kyle Taylor described an incident that occurred on his third day as an administrator:

One of my fourth-grade math teachers was concerned about a "severe deviation from the dress code." I thought perhaps a student was wearing something with inappropriate writing— or worse, nothing at all. The actionable offense: the shape of a star cut into the fade of a young Black male student's hair. K.D. is what he liked to be called. Concerned about K.D. breaking policies guided by our code of conduct, this teacher made sure to find me on my way to lunch duty to report this incident and wrote a note for his conduct folder. She wanted his hair fixed before returning to class. I told her, "Thank you. I will address the issue with the student and their parent."

At lunch, I had the opportunity to sit next to K.D. for a minute or two and we talked about what most fourth-grade boys like to converse about: video games and football. I found out K.D.'s favorite football team was the Dallas Cowboys; earlier that week, he had finished his season with them on his Xbox and had won the Super Bowl, and he was ecstatic. In recognition of his recent victory, he asked his barber to cut a star into his hair to show pride for his favorite team. I asked K.D. if he knew about our school dress code when it came to hair and designs. He shook his head side-to-side because what nine-year-old would? I replied to his response with, "I love your hair, man. And guess what? I'm a Cowboys fan, too." K.D.'s face lit up. "Do me a favor, next time you get your hair cut, let me know, OK? I want a fade as clean as yours." K.D. laughed and said, "I've never seen a white guy in there."

"Think your barber can make me look good?" K.D. shrugged his shoulders, laughed, and said, "Yes, sir."

When lunch was finished, I returned K.D. to class. We fist-bumped as he went to learn more math with his friends. The teacher, visually upset, closed her door and spoke to me in the hallway about how his hair would be a distraction to the learning environment. I asked her to look into the classroom where K.D. was working on his latest project with his group—not a distraction in the world.

I had my haircut that next week with K.D., and he and I have talked Cowboys football weekly.

These two vignettes offer much to analyze about the cultures of these schools, including race, bias, prejudice, and problematic school policies that certainly need to be addressed and changed. We have collective and individual responsibility to address injustice. Kyle clearly has more work to do on school policies and staff issues.

For the purposes of this chapter, I want to focus on the simple interactions—the just teaching interactions—that led to deeper relationships with individual students. These are small interactions around something that others at their schools had overlooked. In addition to being culturally responsive, Cierra and Kyle responded to individuals. As educators, we need to get outside of ourselves and into the worlds of our students. These two educators were genuinely curious about their students' lives, which led them to ask questions. This benefits our students, but do not miss the benefits we receive through these connections. Both Cierra and Kyle connected with other human beings on areas of common interest. Their curiosity allowed them to see the assets their students bring to school each day that enrich the culture and community that educators and students build together to create a verdant ecosystem for learning.

Schools are full of stories like these. Some stories only take a brief conversation. Others take more time and coordinated resources, but they all require us to see students, build our empathic capacity, and make the connections students need to thrive (see Box 2.7 for how to use questions to elicit stories).

2.7 Just Teaching Strategy

Seeing Whole People Through Questions

If you are a genuinely curious person, then this strategy might be obvious to you. Possibly the two greatest learning tools we have as teachers are questions and our ears. Here are a few ideas for how to start some conversations that might help us see whole people.

1. Find some time to see your students outside of your classroom. This could be in the hall, at lunch, at recess (if you have it), or at a school event.

2. Watch how they interact and with whom.

3. What makes you curious about their interactions?

4. What is something that they seem to value?

5. Do you have any common interests? If so, start there. If not, good—you are about to learn from someone who is different from you.

6. Do not fear being awkward or looking ignorant but try to take what you have learned and ask them about something that makes them interesting. If you need a few generic starter questions, try one of these:

    What do you do for fun?

    What kind of music do you like?

    If you had 30 minutes to do whatever you want, what would it be?

Whatever their responses are, do not judge. Remember, you are there to see them as a whole person, so you are learning—not judging.

Empathy as the Goal and Path

What if empathy is the goal as well as the path to that goal? Much of what is required of educators today is empathy. While not new to the human experience, the word *empathy* only became a word in the early 20th century and was originally used to describe how we enter into the emotional experience of viewing a piece of art. This is similar to how we enter into the emotional experience of another as if we are in the same experience.

Empathy as the goal: One of the most influential books on 21st-century education has been *Understanding by Design* by Grant Wiggins and Jay McTighe (2005). They describe seven facets of understanding and list empathy as the highest level of understanding because it requires us to take the perspectives of others. This makes sense as the highest form of understanding because empathy requires us to fully understand a concept from our own vantage point and then see that concept from the perspectives of others.

Empathy as the path: To reach this higher level of understanding, we need to expand our own capacity for empathy. "Empathy is best understood as a human capacity consisting of several different facets [our capacity to perceive, process, and respond to others] that work together to enable us to be moved by the plights and emotions of others" (Riess & Neporent, 2018, p. 10). Unlike *sympathy*, in which we enter into suffering and feel the pain of others, *empathic* capacity allows us to imagine that we are in the same situation without focusing on ourselves. "This distinction is important because it allows you to consider the best way to help this person without focusing solely on your own discomfort" (p. 13). Helen Riess, a Harvard psychiatrist and medical doctor, studies ways to increase our capacity for empathy. She uses an ABC approach that asks us to (A) *acknowledge* we are entering into a difficult conversation or circumstance, (B) take deep *breaths* to manage our reaction, and (C) engage our *curiosity* to learn more (see Box 2.8).

2.8 Just Teaching Strategy

EMPATHY

Dr. Riess identifies seven keys to empathy and uses the word itself as an acronym. Her keys are useful in thinking about how to develop greater empathic capacity without burning ourselves out. Again, this is not about asking for a heaping serving of some new training to add to our already overflowing plates. This is about developing—not diminishing—capacity. In fact, research shows that empathy improves outcomes (Trzeciak & Mazzarelli, 2019) and reduces burnout (Lamothe et al., 2014) due to the spike in endorphins that we get when we help others (Luks, 1998). In essence, we personally benefit when others benefit from our empathy. Obviously, if our only reason to build empathic capacity was to benefit ourselves, that would demonstrate a very low level of empathy, but the benefits of empathy have been empirically proven.

While Dr. Riess focuses her work on the medical profession, educators can apply all of these keys to their interactions with students, families, and each other.

E—Eye contact: Oxytocin is released when people make eye contact, which bonds people together. Riess suggests making eye contact long enough to determine the eye color of the person we are meeting for the first time. This additional split second is enough time to make a useful connection.

M—Muscles of facial expression: The muscles in the face determine the expressions we make and determine how others perceive us and, therefore, require our attention. Riess suggests that we should look at the full face to determine fake and genuine smiles and emotions while attending to our own facial expressions. Mirror neurons cause us to respond unconsciously to others' expressions with those that mirror theirs—a smile elicits a smile and a frown is more likely to elicit a frown. We can use this to our advantage by managing our own expression for maximum communication of empathy.

P—Posture: The way we hold our body communicates a great deal. Are we demonstrating openness, putting ourselves at eye level, and leaning in or are we turning slightly away, folding our arms, and closing ourselves off? Getting to eye level (like a good kindergarten teacher), leaning in, and nodding communicate care and concern to others.

A—Affect: Affect (short a sound) is the scientific word for emotion. Typically, our faces communicate our emotions. In addition to checking for eye color, Riess also makes a habit of identifying the emotional state of each patient when she begins to interact with them. Except in the case where a person's expression is mismatched with their own emotions (which is the case for some people), this could help us as educators to start where students are each day.

T—Tone of voice: Tone of voice includes pace, volume, and pitch. Riess cites research that tone of voice is responsible for 38% of nonverbal communication and is, therefore, a critical component of empathy. Being aware of our tone and the tone of the person to whom we are talking will increase our empathic capacity.

(Continued)

(Continued)

H—Hearing the whole person: As Cierra Nickerson's example at the beginning of this section demonstrates, we need to take time to truly listen in order to hear each person on multiple levels. Riess suggests that we use empathic listening which first tries to understand the other's perspective; after that, we can try to be understood. This requires that we set aside our own emotions and perspectives while we listen in a nonjudgmental way.

Y—Your response: Dr. Riess suggests that we should examine our response to an interaction to determine how effectively we expressed empathy. Generally, if we feel good about an interaction, the other involved parties will as well. If something feels off, then perhaps we did not effectively express empathy.

Questions to consider:

1. How will you develop more empathic capacity in yourself?

2. How will you create conditions for others to develop empathic capacity?

3. How would your classroom or school change if empathic capacity increased?

By increasing our empathic capacity, we are likely to find work more meaningful, as we are wired for relationships that are more than transactions. Most educators I know find their greatest sense of fulfillment in helping others. We begin to burn out when our work becomes transactional, we get bogged down in bureaucratic paperwork, or our relationships with others begin to fray due to neglect or distraction. Empathic capacity leads us to deliver compassion, which can have a calming effect due to its engagement of the parasympathetic nervous system (Stellar et al., 2015). Compassion is a two-way street that benefits both the giver and receiver and is foundational for deeper relationships. Compassion does not have to take additional time. Researchers have found a strong association between doctors exhibiting compassion for as little as 40 seconds and improved health outcomes for patients, including reduced perceptions of pain, depression, and anxiety and improved results for diabetic and cancer patients (Trzeciak & Mazzarelli, 2019). If compassion is associated with these improved outcomes for patients, then (even moving beyond our moral and ethical imperative to demonstrate compassion) we as educators should be demonstrating compassion for our own good and for improved outcomes for our students.

Cookies

Sometimes, small gestures matter the most. When schools and universities shut their doors in the spring of 2020 due to a pandemic, many college students found themselves isolated from friends and family. Some college students could not go home because they were international students and others did not want to expose family members to greater risk. Many of my Baylor students were living alone in off-campus housing and were uncertain about how to get through the rest of the semester. We were able to meet on Zoom, and most of their days were spent on screens as their only windows to a bewildering outside world. My three children were also unable to go to their schools and were home all day as my wife and I tried to continue our work. Our situation was not unique.

My middle school daughter, Grace, walked by my computer screen one day during Zoom class. When the class entered the breakout rooms, she asked, "Where are all of the students living?"

I answered, "Some are back at their families' homes but most of them are still living near campus by themselves or with a roommate."

She immediately announced, "Sarah and I will make them cookies. Can you help us deliver them?"

She and her sister immediately started mixing chocolate chip cookies. In their view, chocolate chip cookies are a panacea for all of the world's ills. We left warm cookies outside the door of each local student that day and let them know they were there. While we could not be in the same physical space at the time, my daughters' chocolate chip cookies were a small encouragement in an uncertain time. Maybe scores on the assignment for the next class went up. I don't remember. However, the cookies communicated that we are all human and that was what mattered. The cookies communicated, "You are not alone. You are seen. You are loved," by two young girls they have never met. We need to Maslow before we Bloom.

Also, maybe the world simply needs more Hope Academies and warm chocolate chip cookies.

Just Teaching Tool #2

Well-being Thermometer

1. Each of the following components contributes to well-being.

2. A healthy temperature is approximately 98 degrees.

3. Rate the following components of well-being from 0–14 (very unscientific and meant to elicit discussion only).

4. Total the number of degrees for each level (class, school, district).

5. Compare results with your colleagues.

6. Where do you agree or disagree? Where can you grow?

TOOL #2 | **WELL-BEING THERMOMETER**

TAKING THE TEMPERATURE OF OUR CLASSES, SCHOOL, AND DISTRICT SUPPORT

RATE THE FOLLOWING COMPONENTS
OF WELL-BEING FROM 0-14

USE YOUR FIRST RESPONSE, NOT INTENDED TO BE SCIENTIFIC

	CLASS	SCHOOL	DISTRICT
LAUGH	_____	_____	_____
PLAY	_____	_____	_____
ELICIT STORIES	_____	_____	_____
MODEL GRATITUDE	_____	_____	_____
CREATE MOMENTS	_____	_____	_____
HAVE FUN	_____	_____	_____
SEE WHOLE PEOPLE	_____	_____	_____
THERMOMETER READING			

A HEALTHY TEMPERATURE IS ~ 98°
TOTAL THE # OF DEGREES OF EACH LEVEL

SCAN THE QR CODE
FOR A FILLABLE PDF

Humans Before Outcomes

3

Humans are a lot more fun than outcomes.

Just Teaching

Chapter 3 "Decomplexified"

- Identify what you and your school are known for. Likely, this will be more than a mission statement.

- Identify what you would like to be known for.

- Establish personal, classroom, and school norms and habits that lead to thriving human beings.
  - Classroom norms
    - Tell students who they are becoming.
    - Be you every day.
    - Connect strangers.
    - Focus on skills, shots, and scrappiness.
    - Invite improvement.
  - Norms beyond the classroom: Integrate life and work.
  - School norms: Celebrate struggle, growth, and flourishing.

Faith

We have a $2,000,000,000,000 problem. That's two trillion dollars.

Economists assert that the disrupted academic learning that occurred through the pandemic will cost students this much in future earnings (Goldhaber et al., 2021), with those types of devastating numbers affecting students of color and other underserved students even more significantly (Dorn et al., 2021).

This is how economists frame problems, and the problems are real. However, as educators, we see humans and not merely outcomes. That is a good thing. This humanizes economics. As educators, we humanize numbers. To celebrate our students' humanity, we must first acknowledge our own.

This chapter has been hard for me to start writing. My mom died three weeks ago, and I have COVID-19. One of the only good things I have observed about suffering is that it builds empathic capacity. I now better understand others who have lost their mothers. I better understand what it is like to try to do meaningful work in isolation through a mild COVID fog. These are not lessons I really wanted to learn, but they are lessons that can make me a better educator and person because I can better see and serve individuals who have been through similar experiences.

Our students bring these experiences into our classrooms every day. How can we see our students as human beings even when we do not have the same experiences they do? Do we have to be lonely to see their loneliness? Can we understand abuse or neglect if we ourselves have not been abused or neglected? I think we can if we are attentive to what they share with us.

One scene from this past year sticks with me: a classroom visit I made in South Carolina that demonstrates how empathy and relationship connect us in ways that we cannot even imagine when we learn about the challenges another person faces. A four-year-old boy was recovering from a seizure on a pad on the floor of the prekindergarten classroom. He had braces on both legs, looked like he weighed about 30 pounds, and had a tiny wheelchair parked next to him. He was making a small noise and making eye contact with his teacher. She walked to him, scooped him up, and held him close as she told me, "Sometimes he just needs some snuggles." While he could not verbally communicate, the smile that lit his face was more than enough confirmation that she was right.

When working with educators, I regularly share a quote attributed to Colleen Wilcox: "Teaching is the greatest act of optimism." Optimism comes from love and a desire to see others thrive. We need faith to believe that we can solve $2,000,000,000,000 problems and that we can meet the needs of each student even through the suffering that we all endure.

What We Know: Beyond Luxury Beliefs and Mission Statements

Luxury beliefs are "ideas and opinions that confer status on the rich at very little cost while taking a toll on the lower class" (Henderson in Pondisco, 2021). Robert Pondisco (2021) writes,

> Nowhere is the gulf between upscale ideals and everyday reality wider or more obvious than in education policy and practice. Too few of us know or have personal experience walking in the shoes of the families and students we claim to serve. Instead, we opine about what's best for other people's children from the safety of our respective bubbles, indulging our own set of luxury beliefs. For example, claiming that teachers in underserved areas are adequately compensated and supported when we are living in suburban enclaves of affluent public schools or sending our children to well-resourced private schools is a luxury belief.

Teachers and administrators are much less likely to hold luxury beliefs because we see the effects of bad policy firsthand. Heather Williams, the 2021 Arkansas Assistant Principal of the Year, shared DeAndre's story, which reinforces our need to understand the backgrounds our students bring into our schools.

> DeAndre is a five-year-old boy who began kindergarten this school year. He started the school year two weeks late. During DeAndre's first week of kindergarten, he screamed and cried more than any other student transitioning into our school environment. His behaviors escalated to throwing objects, pushing over tables, and knocking over chairs. In his first month of kindergarten, DeAndre already had multiple disciplinary referrals due to disruptive, unsafe behaviors. We knew we needed to find a solution to ensure that DeAndre was successful, safe, loved, and engaged while he was in our care at school. Through engaging in multiple conversations with his mom, I learned that she was in the middle of a Department of Human Services open case for child maltreatment and neglect. Her three children were taken from her for six months, and she just got them back in her custody the first week of school. DeAndre's father had been killed in a homicide that DeAndre had witnessed. Upon

learning this information, we were better able to understand the context of trauma that DeAndre had and currently is experiencing.

This understanding allowed teachers and administrators to change their approach in how they served DeAndre.

> We worked hard to partner with his mom to provide support for DeAndre, including counseling services through a local Child Safety Center. We ensured that DeAndre had food sent home weekly. We also realized that he wasn't getting enough sleep at night. Through taking calculated ABC (antecedent, behavior, consequence) data, we realized that the majority of his meltdowns were around the same time of day. This led to us implementing a nap time for DeAndre to help support his well-being while at school. We began to see DeAndre's engagement in learning increase. Over the next two months, DeAndre did not receive a disciplinary referral.

> His teacher, Mrs. Walker, worked so hard throughout this journey to ensure that she had strategies in place to support DeAndre in the classroom. There were times that it was very hard for her to fully engage with DeAndre, especially through the periods of serious disruption. However, the time, support, and true understanding that we spent to understand DeAndre led to improvement for his teacher as well. Mrs. Walker was better able to develop a sense of well-being for herself as well as better engagement with each student.

Based on what you now know about Heather's school through this approach to DeAndre—an approach that is not rooted in luxury beliefs or reductionistic outcomes—how would you characterize the school's mission statement? This is an important question because, for many educators and most students, mission statements are merely words that show up on a website or signage around a school. School improvement teams can spend hours wordsmithing mission statements that attempt to summarize the aims and values of the organization. Sometimes schools think they have a mission statement because there is a catchphrase that everyone repeats. We should be able to see the mission statement in action in the way students and educators interact daily. Try a quick self-assessment in Box 3.1.

3.1 Just Teaching Strategy

What Is Your Mission?

1. What is your school's mission statement? Try to recall this from memory, if possible, or look it up if you are like me and cannot remember it.

2. What percentage of administrators do you think could recite the mission statement?

    Teachers?

    Students?

3. If I walked into your school, what would I say the mission statement is based on the way educators and students interact?

4. In one sentence, based on what you read, what might Heather Williams's school's mission statement be?

5. If you were responsible for your school's mission statement, what would it be?

What Works in Real Schools: Norms for Classrooms, Beyond Classrooms, and Schoolwide

Perhaps we need to rethink what an "effective" school is. Effective schools focus on the academic, social, and emotional development of students. Schools that have this holistic focus increase graduation rates and college completion more than schools that focus primarily on grades (Jackson et al., 2020). Whatever our mission statements say, purpose-driven flourishing should be at the center.

If you are a teacher, you can only control what is within your sphere of influence, so we will start in the classroom to understand purpose-driven flourishing. Your influence extends far beyond the classroom and can be maximized when efforts extend schoolwide. Here are some classroom norms and rituals you can put into place right now that can put humans before outcomes.

Classroom Norm #1: Tell Students Who They Are Becoming

Bob Goff, a lawyer turned inspirational author and speaker, regularly reminds us to tell others who they are becoming—not who we want them to be or who we wish we were. To do this, we need to be able to identify the attributes of each student and then be able to articulate those attributes. Be sure to keep the attributes positive. Goff's point is that we help speak into being the attributes that we see, so going negative does not help anyone.

To know how best to tell students who they are becoming, we do have to remember that all relationships, particularly those of teachers and students, go through stages. Teachers and students go through four discreet stages (modified from Cooper & Simonds, 2007):

1. Initiating: This is our first impression. Much of this will be nonverbal, but we will make many judgments within the first 30 seconds with our students. While these insights can be valuable, this is not the time to make major judgments about who a student is becoming and certainly not the time for definitive pronouncements.

2. Experimenting: This is where we test our students and, more importantly, they test us. How much can they get away with? What are the actual expectations? Is this a safe place to take risks? In the first few weeks of the semester, students are experimenting to see what we are all about, and we are testing them to see what they are capable of accomplishing. This is still not the ideal time for making significant pronouncements about who students are, but we are certainly making and testing hypotheses.

3. Deepening: Most of the year is a mix of experimenting and deepening. The sooner students feel like they know what they can expect from us, the deeper the relationship can go. We know how to encourage, exhort, and motivate, and they know who we are as educators. While the relationship is deepening, we should have multiple opportunities to tell students who they are becoming.

4. Morphing: The end of the school year is always filled with melancholy for me. We are no longer a class, and in some ways, the teacher–student relationship ends. I prefer to think of the relationship as morphing as opposed to ending. For most of us who do not loop with our students, they will be in many other classes the following year. We need some closure so that we can move into a new phase of relationship that is more collegial. This is different with a fifth grader than it is with a graduate student, but we get one last chance at the end of the year to tell our students who we see them becoming. We can approach that in different ways. For me, this means each student gets a book with

an inscription inside. When I taught younger students, it was a portfolio of their work, pictures from the year, and a handwritten letter. We need to communicate how we have seen them grow and who we sec them becoming.

To help tell students who they are becoming, try Box 3.2.

3.2 Just Teaching Strategy

Tell Students Who They Are Becoming

1. Pick one student, preferably one with whom you are struggling to connect. Feel free to go back to the "Four Lenses" tool at the end of Chapter 1.

2. What relational stage are you in? (Circle one.)
   Initiating   Experimenting   Deepening   Morphing

3. If you are at Stage 1 or 2, what else do you need to know about the student to know who they are as a person? How might you deepen your relationship to better understand them?

4. If you are at Stage 3 or 4, what is one attribute you can celebrate?

5. How can you share that attribute with them?

Classroom Norm #2: Be Real

I grew up in a small town in Indiana (think Hawkins, Indiana, from *Stranger Things*). When I was in seventh grade, I wanted to be Lance Parker. He was the best basketball player in the grade above me, had perfectly feathered and mulleted hair, always had a comb sticking out of his back pocket, was typically wearing any one of a rainbow of Coca-Cola rugbies, and was trailed by adoring middle school girls. You knew you were in the presence of greatness when you called out, "Hey Lance!" with a tinge of middle school desperation. You knew that you could not hope for an audible greeting much less your name, but maybe he would deign to give you a head nod.

I have no idea what happened to Lance, but I know many of our students have aspirations of being someone else. Sadly, many of us can fall victim to this same desire of being someone else—like the cool English language arts teacher down the hall who has five or six students hanging out in his room after composing slam poetry or your colleague who is the Joanna Gaines of classroom interior design—but this is doomed to failure.

Be the best version of yourself. This sounds trite and relatively cheesy, but this is so essential and there is no other way to say it. If you love *Abbott Elementary,* Jane Austen novels, the Chicago Cubs, Wordle, cooking, or Star Trek, let your students see this about you. They need to know you love them, but they also need to know what else you love. You are uniquely you; by teaching from that identity, you communicate that your students can also be themselves.

Be the best version of yourself *every day* (see Box 3.3). This is not another task or a mask to put on each day. This is much more similar to the app BeReal than Instagram. Instagram is a curated, polished view of our world that leads to crushing comparisons when reality cannot hold up against the unreality of filters, performance, and selective disclosure. Millions of high school and college students are using BeReal to celebrate more of who they really are each day. Once a day, BeReal notifies users to upload a picture of what they are doing at that moment—no filters and no reality-altering narratives. To see anyone else's post, the user has to post first. This is liberating.

We can speak, act, and teach in ways that give life or suck the soul out of it. Our students deserve a consistent, positive constant in their lives and that can be us. When I am the best version of myself and teaching from my own identity, I am much more likely to find joy consistently. When I taught science to middle school students, I did not always feel like the best version of myself at the beginning of a day or class period. However, my students deserved the best version of a science teacher I could be, and I was only as good as my worst day. The good news is that even when I did not always feel like the best version of myself, reminding myself that my students deserved my best would enhance my well-being and improve my teaching.

3.3 Just Teaching Strategy

Be Real

When are you at your best as a teacher or administrator?

What are three words that students would use to describe you when you are at your best?

If there are 40 hours in each week (I know you want a job in that school where the job is only 40 hours!), how many of those hours are you at your best?

What do you need to do to be the best version of yourself more consistently?

Classroom Norm #3: Connect Strangers

Especially when we teach in kindergarten, large middle schools, sprawling high schools, or any school with high levels of transience, we are connecting strangers. If the primary reason kids do not like school is loneliness (Brooks, 2021), then teaching strangers is an essential skill we have to master. I make it a practice to memorize all my students' names on the first day of class regardless of the class size, which for me has never been more than 100. If I have access to their pictures in our learning management system before the semester, I study them for the week or two leading up to the first day. Then I visualize students' names written on their foreheads and use their names as frequently as I can during the first class. They cannot leave until I have called each one by name from memory. The logic here is that everyone is gracious on the first day. While it is an ambitious goal to do this the first day and you might not always achieve it, at least you will be well on your way. What is unforgivable is not knowing names after the first few weeks.

A name gives us an entry point into a relationship. A name does not constitute a relationship but it is typically a precondition. I have also realized that it is not enough for me to be the only one who knows all the names in a class, because we are not a community if we do not know each other at least by name. One of the things that always surprises me about college classrooms is how few students know each other's names. That is why I use Paideia seminar (see Box 3.4).

3.4 Just Teaching Strategy

Paideia Seminar
http://www.paideia.org/

These seminars run from 30–45 minutes and require students to build on the ideas of others while giving attribution. The facilitator's job is to ask questions and take notes on the conversation marking each contribution. Several steps precede a Paideia seminar.

1) As a group, we select one goal from this list:

- All comments will be text-based.
- Ask clarifying questions.
- Create space for everyone to share.
- Allow 10 seconds of silence after a question has been posed.
- Build on others' ideas.

(Continued)

(Continued)

2) Individually, students select one personal goal from this list:

- To focus on the speaker (listen)

- To speak at least three times

- To ask at least two questions

- To refer to the text at least twice

- To take notes on others' comments

- To use "I" statements during the seminar

3) Students write their names on a name tent in large, bold letters so that everyone can read their names in class. This is important so that students can build on others' ideas and ensure that they all feel connected.

4) On the back of the name tent are two sets of reminders:

- SLANT: sit up, listen, ask/answer questions, nod, track the speaker

- Sentence starters to help students who struggle with how to enter the conversation:

    o "I want to add"

    o "I have a different idea about"

    o "I have a question about"

    o "I disagree with the statement"

    o "The text says"

    o "I've changed my mind about"

5) As a facilitator, I always prepare at least six to eight questions. The first two questions are round-robin questions that require every participant to answer. These are typically questions such as, "What is a word, phrase, or sentence that best describes X?" The initial questions are important for engaging each student. The next four to six questions are open to anyone and drive toward a deeper collective understanding.

6) Throughout the seminar, students have to build on each other's ideas and use each other's names. Therefore, every student has a name tent. After the seminar, students reflect on their success as

a group and as an individual. Then students complete a writing
assignment of 400 words or less that synthesizes their thinking on
the topic. The writing is always better after a Paideia seminar and
the class is more connected because we know each other more fully.

Based on grade level, the expectations for writing could certainly
be adjusted.

Classroom Norm #4: Focus on Skills, Shots, and Scrappiness

If I were to distill just teaching into one phrase, it would be to give each
student what they need. This is justice. This is just teaching. In his book,
Outliers, Malcolm Gladwell (2008) asserts that people are successful
when they have skill, opportunity, and grit. To "Hamiltonize" that, students need skill, a shot, and scrappiness.

- Skill—We all need some baseline level of skill to be successful.
  Alexander Hamilton definitely had a solid baseline that he developed
  in school, business, and the law. As educators, we also have to have
  some baseline skills in a pedagogical content area and with people.

- Shot—Lin Manuel Miranda's Alexander Hamilton raps
  eloquently about his desire for a shot. He wants the opportunity
  to be successful. As educators, we get to connect students with
  opportunities. Allowing students to work on real-world problems,
  connect with experts, or serve their communities gives them the
  opportunity to connect with something bigger.

- Scrappiness—Alexander Hamilton was nothing if not "young,
  scrappy, and hungry." He outwrote, outworked, and outhustled
  everyone. No one succeeds without some level of skill, but as
  Angela Duckworth (2016) points out, effort counts twice as we
  develop skill. We need some baseline level of talent with which
  we exert effort to initially develop a skill, then we take that skill,
  apply effort, and achieve. Consider teaching as an example. We
  need some talent for a subject and the ability to work with others.
  We exert effort to enhance both our pedagogical knowledge of the
  subject and the knowledge of those we are teaching, which results
  in some level of skill. We continue to develop our teaching skills
  with effort, which leads to better achievement for our students.

Giving each student what they need means developing skills, giving
them a shot, and helping them develop scrappiness. This does not

mean that we can intrinsically motivate students because, by definition, intrinsic motivation must come from *within* the student. As educators, we create conditions where students can develop skills, have an opportunity, and develop a passion that can lead to scrappiness (see Box 3.5).

3.5 Just Teaching Strategy

Creating Conditions

How effective are you at creating conditions for students?

1) On a scale of 0–10, how would you rate your classroom for creating conditions where students can develop skills?

   0 = "I am happy if students show up."

   10 = "Students are constantly refining meaningful life and academic skills."

2) On a scale of 0–10, how would you rate your classroom or school for creating conditions where students have a shot?

   0 = "My students need to earn their shot before I give it to them."

   10 = "Every student is challenged every day with growth opportunities that build expertise."

3) On a scale of 0–10, how would you rate your classroom or school for creating conditions where students can develop scrappiness?

   0 = "I want to make everything easy for students so they can all get a trophy."

   10 = "We celebrate hard-won growth every day."

Total score: _____

How effective is your classroom at creating positive conditions?

When you rate your school on these questions, are your personal score and your school's score aligned?

When you do this activity in a professional learning community, how does your score compare to the scores of your colleagues?

Classroom Norm #5: Invite Improvement

As we become more comfortable in our own skins as teachers, inviting improvement gets easier. Christopher Emdin's (2016) cogenerative dialogue technique has become a favorite in my practice over the past five years. I have used this at all levels of teaching and am convinced that it is one of the fastest ways to improve classrooms for students. See Box 3.6 for specific directions on how to use this technique.

Using cogenerative dialogues, I have improved presentations, assignments, and my communication and have modeled a tool for leaders to invite improvement. As we do this together, we are improving our classes and making it OK to ask others for critical feedback that is solution oriented. No longer am I solely responsible for the way our class works. This is liberating and is a manifestation of confident humility—having faith in ourselves while knowing we might not yet have the right solution (Grant, 2021).

3.6 Just Teaching Strategy

Cogenerative Dialogues (Emdin, 2016)

1) Identify four students of diverse backgrounds and abilities.

2) Approach the four students as you would a colleague. "I need two to three minutes of your time. When might be good for you?" This is important as you are treating them as colleagues seeking improvement.

3) Set up a space where you can meet in a circle as equals before class, after class, or during lunch for no more than two or three minutes.

4) At your first meeting, tell them, "I'd like you to be a secret board who is going to help me improve our class." The "secret" portion is for their benefit so that they do not take any undue grief for helping you as the teacher.

5) Pick something small that could improve in one week (e.g., "How could we improve the beginning or end of the class?")

6) Listen. Everyone has to speak. Only one person speaks at a time. Do not take suggestions personally or respond defensively.

(Continued)

(Continued)

7) Meet again the following week to discuss progress and tackle another issue.

8) After three weeks, ask one student to bring a friend.

9) The following week, the student who invited the friend rotates off and is a secret ally to help the class run more smoothly.

10) After three weeks, ask another student to bring a friend and repeat the rotation to increase the investment of members of the class.

Elevating Norms and Habits to Rituals

"Our rituals are habits with a soul" (McKeown, 2021, p. 51). The end-of-chapter tool asks you to consider habits and norms you can develop in your classroom or school. We elevate habits and norms by creating rituals.

Here are a couple of examples that represented Friday rituals for my classes. At 3:15 on Friday afternoon, our work would be over for the week if we had been productive all week. We kept track of our level of engagement all week with a magnetic Elvis on the board who came complete with a variety of outfits. If all of Elvis's clothing and accessories were intact at 3:15, the last 15 minutes of the day were reserved for class kickball. This time was sacred, especially for me—a huge kickball aficionado.

The second Friday ritual was that all the week's work would be graded and returned on Friday. Typically, 10–13 assignments would go home in the Friday folder. That meant Thursday nights and Friday lunches were busy, but it also ensured that (1) grading did not pile up for me and (2) students could end the week with a mini celebration of all they had learned.

These rituals look different at every grade level and in different contexts, but finding ways to elevate norms to rituals increases their meaning and enhances joy.

Beyond the Classroom: Work–Life Integration

Do you know anyone who has found work–life balance? I know a lot of people who are looking for it, but I cannot think of anyone who claims to have achieved it. That seems like a problem. Please read the section with caution. I am not suggesting that this is another set of things that you need to do when you are already stretched to a breaking point. Depending on your life circumstances, some of these suggestions might not be viable or even possible for you. These are simply a few ways I have seen work and life beyond work be mutually enriching.

We can learn a lot from fields other than education. On a recent *Freakonomics* podcast, the host Steven Dubner (2020) asked a critical care doctor what he says when he has to deliver hard news to a patient. Here is the interchange:

> Dubner: Can you give me an example or two of something that you say that you wouldn't have said? Or maybe it's something that you say differently? Is it the way you touch someone that you might not have touched before? Is it eye contact?

> Dr. Stephen Trzeciak: Actually, it's not something that I say. Oftentimes it's something that I don't say. It's just being present. I practice critical care and there are a lot of times when the outcome is not something that can be changed. And sometimes you just need to sit with people and their suffering. "You're not going to go through this alone." "I am here with you."

This is not only true when we are delivering bad news. We need to be present for our students—certainly during the school day and, when possible, outside the school day. In addition to feeding our genuine curiosity about who our students are outside the classroom, investing time in students lets them know that we value them. When I first began teaching, I lived on the 17th floor of an apartment complex that housed many of my students. For many teachers, that might sound like a significant impediment to separating life from work, but I have found that the best way for me to find balance is to integrate my life, family, and work.

Instead of work–life balance, what if we aspire to work–life integration? We do not really have two separate lives anyway—one for work and one for life. Why not integrate work and life in mutually beneficial ways? As educators, I think this might be possible when it comes to spending time that we do not have to spend contractually. Here are a few ideas that have worked for me over the years. (Please remember the earlier warning. Depending on your life circumstances, these might be more or less viable, and only do them if they seem like they would benefit both your work and life!)

1) **Make it a date.** My wife and I go to middle school and high school performances as dates. Some of our least expensive and

most fun dates have been going to high school musicals, middle school plays, talent shows, recitals, or games—high school football games in Texas are the civic events of the year. Now we take our kids to these events even when they are not performing so they can appreciate others' talents. On a teacher's budget, these kinds of dates and family events are cheap, fun ways to connect life and work.

2) **Be strategic.** If we know something is going on nearby, I will grab one of my kids and tell them we are going to stop by an event for 15 minutes and then get dinner or a smoothie if they will go with me. This gives me a chance to connect with one of my own children and show up for my students.

3) **Make an investment you enjoy.** I coached girls' and boys' basketball and tennis for years. I love both sports and know how to teach both—and basketball and tennis bring me joy. Coaching was not a sacrifice, as it was usually a life-giving experience for me that energized me and allowed me to connect with students and my own children.

4) **Let students connect with you and your family.** When I was single and living in the apartment complex, I saw my students everywhere. They knew when I was at the pool, when I was working out, and when I was at the store. Admittedly, not everyone would see this as a positive. However, they saw me as a real person who was living with three other guys. After I married my wife and began to have kids of my own, I started teaching college students. One of the greatest blessings of my work with college students has been the students who have walked alongside us in life. Students have lived with us when they have had housing needs, babysat for us, and spent countless hours and meals with our family. We still play games that students introduced to us on class/family game nights. Obviously, teaching adult college students is different than teaching younger students, but creating points of connection is mutually beneficial.

If we are interested in the holistic development of students, then we have to connect with whole individuals and they need to see that we are also whole. This has to function as a continuum based on the age of our students and the demands of our families, but integrating work and life in ways that enhance connections between the significant relationships in our lives can be socially and emotionally healthy (see Box 3.7).

3.7 Just Teaching Strategy

Work–Life Integration Audit

What are opportunities for integrating work and life in ways that could be life-giving to you and your students? Only do things that are life-giving here. Do not add anything that drains your energy.

Work:

1) What do you enjoy doing outside of school time that your students also enjoy?

2) Are there students with whom you really need to connect?

   a. Are there school-sponsored teams or clubs that you could sponsor, lead, and enjoy?

   b. Are there easy opportunities to watch students perform?

   c. Do you have friends or family members who might enjoy attending a particular event with you?

Life:

1) What is the best aspect of your life right now?

   a. How could you enhance this aspect of your life with anything happening at school?

2) What feels stale or routine?

   a. How could work create opportunities for connections or experiences that could make life more interesting?

Integration:

1) What is one step you could take to integrate work and life in a way that could be mutually beneficial to your life and work?

2) When will you take this step?

3) Who do you need to include in this step?

Schoolwide Efforts: What Does Your School Celebrate?

Burnout is the enemy of well-being. We cannot lead for well-being by ourselves. Collective leadership is the work of teachers and leaders toward shared goals (Eckert, 2018). The efforts of individuals are most effective when they are part of a broader effort because "a bad system will beat a good person every time" (Deming, 1993). We cannot add leadership and well-being to the plate of educators who are already overwhelmed with the demands placed on them. Our efforts must be collective *and* based on an ethic of care. "Caring is not a specific domain of leadership, nor is it a discrete set of leadership strategies. It is a quality or property of leadership generally" (Smylie et al., 2020, p. 33). The good news is that caring, collective leadership is not something additional that needs to be done. Caring is the way we do our work, does not necessarily take additional time, and is life-giving to those who serve and are served.

One of my favorite questions to ask school leaders across the country is this: What do you celebrate? When the response centers on a bond effort, a building, or a technology initiative, I become a bit concerned. How would you answer (see Box 3.8)?

3.8 Just Teaching Strategy

Celebrate Care

You are about to read several examples of schools that care well for their students and tell stories of that care to celebrate, remember, and cultivate culture. Take a few moments to reflect on what you, your class, and your school have celebrated in the past year:

1. What is something that administrators at your school have celebrated?

2. What is something that teachers at your school have celebrated?

3. What is something that students at your school have celebrated?

Now think about how your school community has demonstrated care this past year:

1. What is the best example you have seen of someone caring for another?

2. How was it celebrated? How could it be celebrated?

We do not celebrate care to create an incentive for people to care. We celebrate caring so that others recognize what is happening and so that we can give them a model for how to do this well. We replicate what we celebrate.

When I see eyes well up and hear stories of lives that are changed because of the work occurring in schools and communities, I know that I am about to hear about the magic that happens in schools; however, it is not magic—it is the result of the hard work of educators and students who care. Here are a few snippets from my field notes:

> "Two student leaders prayed on another student's porch for his mother who was in isolation as she prepared for surgery to address cancer."

> "A team of students formed a tech support hotline for students struggling with technology issues at home."

> "Teams of teachers and administrators delivered yard signs and meals to students who could not come to school due to health concerns."

> "Over the last ten years, a student-run coffee cart has become a test kitchen, greenhouse, and organic farm that is now serving students and the community."

These are the things that we should be celebrating. We should be celebrating Juan (pseudonym) and Mr. Jackson. Tamela Crawford, a Texas assistant superintendent, shared their story:

> Juan was a seventh-grade student who has experienced significant trauma from a very young age. He came from a home filled with domestic violence and exposure to drugs. Thankfully, he had a strong support system with his grandmother.

> At the age of six, Juan's grandmother was granted full custody by the courts, and he began to flourish in elementary school. Teachers and classmates knew of Juan's situation and wanted to help this outgoing, vibrant boy. His teachers and campus administration took a significant interest in him and provided opportunities for him, and he was successful. I guess you could consider Juan a success story.

> At the end of Juan's sixth-grade year, his grandmother was diagnosed with cancer. Having come from a turbulent childhood and fearful of losing his grandmother, Juan

felt obligated to care for her. As a seventh-grade student, Juan completely disengaged from school and rarely came. His grades were dismal and his bright future was beginning to dim.

Our assistant principal, Mr. Jackson, took notice and when Juan made it to campus, Mr. Jackson would intentionally interact with Juan each day. When Juan was not on campus, Mr. Jackson would conduct home visits and bring him to school. Mr. Jackson initiated our student assistance team meetings to ensure that teachers and counselors were aware of the situation and collaborated with them to create a support system that provided the services needed for Juan to thrive while he was on campus.

In the summer of Juan's eighth-grade year, his grandmother was successfully treated for her cancer, and it was as if the weight of the world had been lifted from Juan's shoulders. Mr. Jackson knew he needed to get Juan's new teachers together to create a plan to ensure Juan's success for the upcoming school year, and on the first day of school, Mr. Jackson was at the bus drop off ready to see Juan step off the bus. Each day, Mr. Jackson was there waiting for Juan. Juan had a great year that year and continues to do well in high school. Mr. Jackson continues to check in on Juan and his grandmother.

Our care extends to entire systems and over many years. We need more Mr. Jacksons and more success stories like Juan's. Juan's story is far from over, but stories like his build gritty optimism that is grounded in reality rather than naivete. What a blessing it is to be transformed by the work that changes the trajectory of lives, and it's not bad for students either. We get a lot better outcomes when our outcomes are humans.

TOOL #3 | **NORM GENERATOR**

BUILD NORMS THAT CREATE THRIVING COMMUNITIES

ANSWER THE QUESTIONS IN EACH CATEGORY BELOW AND RECORD ONE NORM YOU WANT TO ENACT

YOU

1. 3 words that describe the best version of you.
2. What habits help you be the best version?
3. How are you inviting improvement?

∨

NEW NORM

CLASS

1. What skills do students develop in class?
2. What shots do students get in your class?
3. What norms develop scrappiness?

∨

NEW NORM

COMMUNITY

1. 3 words others would use to describe your school.
2. For what is your school known?
3. For what would you like your school to be?

∨

NEW NORM

SCHOOL

1. What does your school celebrate?
2. How do school leaders invite improvement?
3. How do you all integrate work and life?

∨

NEW NORM

ENACT THESE NEW NORMS, *STARTING WITH YOU.*

SCAN THE QR CODE
FOR A FILLABLE PDF

Part II

Engagement

The next two chapters explore how we can fully engage our students. Engagement flows from and contributes to well-being. Engagement is a prerequisite for meaningful feedback because without engagement, neither one matter.

FEEDBACK, **ENGAGEMENT**, & WELL-BEING

WELL-BEING
PURPOSE-DRIVEN FLOURISHING

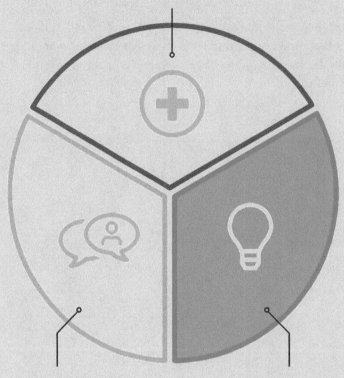

FEEDBACK
PURPOSE-DRIVEN
WISDOM FOR GROWTH

ENGAGEMENT
CONTENT, CONSOLIDATION,
COLLABORATION, CREATION

Cs Before As

4

Engagement is the heart of teaching and the lifeblood of learning.

Just Teaching

Chapter 4. "Decomplexified"

- Engagement is about finding joy.

- Engagement requires four Cs: content, consolidation, collaboration, and creation.

- In schools, we can use a wide range of tools to address the four Cs:

  - Content: High-quality materials are personalized to each student, are organized, are contextualized, and are appropriately challenging.

  - Consolidation: Students need to be able to review and retrieve learning on a regular basis through friendly competition and study that allows them to have multiple exposures to content and to track their progress.

  - Collaboration: Through low-tech and high-tech tools, students and teachers collaborate to apply and synthesize their learning in ways that lead to "burstiness."

  - Creation: The ultimate goal of our teaching should be for students to engage in tasks that allow them to create work that is meaningful and demonstrates their skills and knowledge.

- Before grading, ensure students are engaged.

Digestive Engagement

Every year that I taught seventh-grade science, we finished our state-prescribed curriculum by February. We were able to do this through effective assessment (see Chapters 6 and 7) and efficient lesson planning. Except for a one-week review of seventh-grade standards before the state exam, we were able to spend March through May studying additional science concepts that we thought seventh graders should know.

This was my favorite time of year because it was as if we had a blank canvas on which to paint our learning. We would build rockets and cars powered by carbon dioxide and conduct inquiry projects based on students' research questions. We could explore anatomy, physiology, physics, and chemistry—not because it was required by state policy but simply because we wanted to learn more about how the human body works or how we fit into the world around us. Seventh graders, like most of us, are extremely egocentric and are fascinated by anything that involves them—even how the human body engages in the daily process of digestion that results in feces.

The digestive demonstration was always memorable. To build anticipation for how great it would be to get to seventh-grade science, we would allow kindergartners to join us for our journey through 24 hours of eating that we would condense into 51 minutes. Because I worked in a K–8 building, the kindergarten teacher would use a trip to the seventh-grade science lab as a reward for students who had done good work throughout the month and would send three to four students up to our lab for the digestive demo. While the kindergarten teacher was happy that her students were rewarded with extension learning, I was thrilled because inviting them into the lab served to build anticipation for what they would experience in seven more years. The kindergartners were always more willing to function as peristalsis and move the food through the stocking that functioned as the large intestine to remove water from the waste. Their eyes lit up when they operated the blender that served as the mouth. The squeals of joy and sense of awe accompanied the chanting of vocabulary and looks of abject horror on green faces of my students due to the smell of expired food and acid. Their visit added to the sense that we were going to celebrate learning that day and made our classes even more engaged in the experience.

To ensure that the focus is on learning, there are clear guidelines for the digestive demo (see the boxed text for the lesson). We only use the scientific name for parts and processes. We repeat the process three times because we typically eat three meals a day and the repetition solidifies the terms and processes in students' minds. I steel my mind against my sophomoric tendency to laugh at bathroom humor. Within 51 minutes, students have a clear understanding of how their own digestive systems work and the vocabulary to describe the parts and processes.

Digestive Demonstration Lesson Plan

Objective:

Students will describe the processes and parts of the digestive system using appropriate vocabulary.

Materials:

- Leftover foods to constitute three meals
- Blender
- Gallon-sized baggies labeled *stomach* and *small intestines*
- Beakers
  - Water with green food coloring for *amylase* (an enzyme in saliva that breaks down carbohydrates)
  - Vinegar with red food coloring for *hydrochloric acid*
  - Water with yellow food coloring for *bile*
- Nylon stocking
- Basin
- Scissors

Procedure:

1) Assign a student to label parts with one color and processes with another on a screen while students complete their own diagram.

2) Ask "Where does digestion begin?"

   Mouth (*mastication*)

   Salivary glands (*amylase*)

3) **Place breakfast in the blender** with amylase and masticate.

4) Pour blended food into the esophagus. This is a paper towel tube labeled *esophagus*. As the food moves through the tube, have students simulate a squeezing motion with their hands and repeat *peristalsis*.

(Continued)

(Continued)

5) From the esophagus, food goes into a gallon-sized baggie labeled *stomach*. Add hydrochloric acid and bile. Have a student gently churn the food by squeezing the outside of the baggie. Be sure it is sealed!

6) After "4 hours" (in the simulation, one minute can equal an hour), pour the *chyme* from the stomach to the bag labeled *small intestines*. Set aside.

7) **Lunch—repeat the process.**

8) Discuss the small intestine: It is approximately 21 feet long in adults (15 feet in 10-year-olds) and composed of villi that remove nutrients. With breakfast and lunch in the small intestine baggie, have a student come up and push their fingers into the outside of the bag to simulate the villi facilitating the transfer of nutrients to the bloodstream.

9) **Dinner—repeat the process.**

10) Discuss the large intestine: It is about 3 feet long and removes water; diarrhea occurs when it is not functioning properly. The total process typically takes 18–24 hours on average from eating to exit.

11) Pour the contents of the small intestine into the nylon hose that simulates the large intestine over a basin. Ask a student to simulate peristalsis by squeezing the large intestine in a gentle, wavelike motion. When most of the water is removed, have another student cut an anus in the nylon and release "*feces*" into the basin.

Assessment: Submit the complete diagram, including a description of the digestive process with correct terminology, and add five bonus points to any student who brings the lab sheet back the next day with a parent/guardian's signature that signifies that the student explained the process to them.

A mentor once told me, "If you have to spend 90% of your lesson getting students engaged before digging deeper into content, then that is what you need to do. If students are not engaged, it does not matter what you are doing."

Engagement is not about entertainment—simply doing what students want us to do.

Engagement is not about compliance—simply getting students to do what we want them to do.

Engagement is about finding joy in learning for both teachers and students.

We have to invite students into that joy by finding what appeals to them. Our family's dog, Charlie, has many skills—spinning, sitting, and shaking hands. We used incentives to teach him these skills. An apple does not work as motivation, but he will run through a wall for a piece of hot dog. I love apples. Charlie does not. When I am teaching Charlie a new skill, it does not matter what I like. What matters is what will invite Charlie to learn. I am not equating our students with Charlie, but the point is that we have to invite students into learning based on what is appealing to them. We can do that through the four Cs that make meaningful engagement possible.

What We Know: The Four Cs—Content, Consolidation, Collaboration, Creation

In the spirit of "decomplexifying" engagement, after years of teaching and supporting teaching, the essence of engagement is *content, consolidation, collaboration,* and *creation.* I will explain this in more detail below, but the lesson plan above demonstrates the four Cs. The *content* was the parts and processes of the digestive system delivered through an in-person demonstration. *Consolidation* happened by repeating the processes through three meals and collectively repeating the terms. *Collaboration* occurred when sharing the digestive process as an entire class, discussing in small and large groups, and asking for simulation volunteers. Content *creation* (no, I am not considering the creation of feces to be content creation) occurred later when students designed their own anatomy inquiry projects. These four areas are comprehensive and move from basic to interesting and complex (see Figure 4.1). Through surveys, conversations, research, and my own practice, I believe that everything we do to engage students in these ways helps us experience the joy that purpose-driven learning can bring.

FIGURE 4.1   The Four Cs of Engagement

CONTENT ⟩ CONSOLIDATION ⟩ COLLABORATION ⟩ CREATION

Content can be tricky because most of what we teach is driven by standards, scope and sequence, and requirements that others place on our classrooms. My opportunity to teach beyond standards every March through May was only possible because I had figured out how to make the content from the state engaging enough through labs and other learning experiences that students were able to master it. As the professionals in the room, we should never complain about the content we are teaching. Our job is to find ways to make the content accessible and engaging to each student. The job is as simple and as complicated as that. To drive deeper learning, we need to structure content in a way that builds ratio (Lemov, 2021). *Building ratio* is increasing the amount of time that students interact with content through questioning, writing, and discussion. We need to move away from covering content to uncovering content (Wiggins & McTighe, 2005) through deeper learning that is responsive to students' experiences and perspectives (Fullan et al., 2018; Hammond, 2015; McTighe & Silver, 2020).

Consolidation is one of my favorite aspects of teaching. Students are beginning to grasp key concepts and then we give them a chance to consolidate what they have learned. We can do this in the form of review games (see Chapter 2) and any form of practice that requires students to retrieve and apply knowledge. Retrieval practice, especially practice that is spaced out or interleaved, significantly enhances performance on assessments and increases the likelihood that concepts will be stored in long-term memory (Brown et al., 2014; Karpicke, 2012).

Collaboration is one of the most valuable skills we can develop in our students for a world that is increasingly interconnected and interdependent while also being increasingly polarized. Students in collaborative classrooms achieve better results on standardized tests and get better grades, and cooperative learning beats traditional learning in an analysis of 65 well-designed research studies (Kyndt et al., 2013). Well-structured collaboration with clear criteria for success and realistic parameters makes our teaching far easier because we are able to distribute how students will receive feedback that will reduce the burden on us. As Robyn Jackson (2009) writes, we should "never work harder than our students" (title page). No longer are we the lone purveyors of knowledge, success, and feedback. Through collaboration, students can improve their work together once we have identified shared goals and what success will look like. (See Chapters 6 and 7 for more.) When it is done well, collaboration between teachers and students and students and other students facilitates perspective-taking that builds empathic capacity in students feeding students' well-being (see Chapters 2 and 3). Empathy through perspective-taking represents the highest level of understanding and should be one of our primary goals as educators (McTighe & Silver, 2020; Wiggins & McTighe, 2005). Additionally, by collaborating with other people, we get the benefit of what Annie Murphy Paul (2021) calls *the extended mind*. She refers to a group mind through transactive memory in which members of a group have their own specialty. No one in the group can remember everything, but by tracking what everyone knows, we know more as a group.

Creation is where teaching and learning fully merge. When students begin to apply and synthesize skills, knowledge, and habits of mind to create new content, novel products, and innovative ways of doing things, schools become vibrant, exciting places that show evidence of collective flourishing. Regardless of the level of students we teach, we should be building skills that help them become writers, mathematicians, scientists, and historians in age-appropriate ways. The best way to do this is to scaffold work so they are using disciplinary tools to develop work that is meaningful to them and demonstrates deepening understanding and skill. The way we get to deeper learning is through more meaningful doing. In his best-selling book, aptly titled *Why Don't Students Like School* (2009), cognitive scientist Dan Willingham describes schools in which students do not create and are forced into one compliance-driven task after another. For the sake of us all, I hope that we are moving in the direction of deeper learning so we can assess and celebrate what students are able to create (Emdin, 2016; Fullan et al., 2018; Hammond, 2015; McTighe & Silver, 2020).

What Works in Real Schools: The Four Cs Applied
Content

One of our primary jobs is to make our content inviting to our students. This does not mean we stand up in front of a class and tell students, "I am really excited about what we are going to learn today. We are talking about end punctuation!" Sadly, I did not make this up—a beginning teacher once shared this with me as his hook to get students engaged in his lesson. Our job is to help the content speak to each student and answer the following questions:

> Why do I want to learn this?
>
> How will this help me?
>
> Why is this relevant to me?
>
> Am I capable of success?

What is a simple, low-tech solution for how to engage students in a lesson on end punctuation? Give students a paragraph without any end punctuation and ask them to try to read it aloud. They will begin to value end punctuation very quickly as they realize its purpose through the four questions above.

One brief caution: Engagement is not about digital technology. This is particularly important because the tools I share in this chapter will change and will be replaced with better tools possibly by the time you are reading this. I am going to share a number of digital tools, but the best engagement I observe and have experienced is through relationships in real-world classrooms. Students are best engaged by teachers who care deeply for them, use humor, and know how to make content accessible. None of this requires technology. However, digital technology can be a tool for deepening our relationships, using humor, and making content accessible. Additionally, I will always end each section with an analog example.

The good news is that we have more tools than ever before to make content accessible and engaging and these tools are improving all the time. I will share a few representative examples here, but the point is not the tool itself. The point is that tools can help us deliver content that is engaging and facilitates the flourishing of each student. The point is that we bring to bear all the resources we have to allow each student to thrive. As the professionals in the room, it is our job to educate ourselves on the best tools available and connect students with the ones that will be most beneficial for them. Here are a few representative tools:

- One great example is Newsela. Newsela is a platform that provides articles written at a range of Lexile levels (a numeric representation of a text's readability) so that students reading at several different levels can read and discuss the same article. The content and graphics are the same, but the text complexity is written at the appropriate level for each reader. Newsela also offers many articles in Spanish at different Lexile levels. This kind of technology is a game-changer. We do not have to spend hours struggling to find reading material on a similar topic but at different reading levels for each student or leveling books with different color dots or collecting book order forms to try to get sets of free books. We do not have to convince intermediate and middle school students that it is OK to read the right level book even if it doesn't look like it is at grade level. Newsela provides the appropriate Lexile level for each student on a common topic so that discussion can happen seamlessly with students contributing from text based on two different languages and variable reading levels.

- We also have incredible digital libraries available on sites such as Epic and CommonLit. Epic provides free access to books, audiobooks, and videos, particularly for elementary-age students and families. CommonLit provides lesson plans, over 2,000 reading passages, and progress trackers for teachers and students in Grades 3–12. Access to digital libraries such as these opens up opportunities, particularly for underserved students, to explore a world of literacy that might not have been as accessible.

- The content resources are not only for reading and writing. Many tools work for all subject areas. We have free tools such as Pear Deck and EdPuzzle that can make our content interactive. Pear Deck makes Google Slides interactive and EdPuzzle allows us to place discussion or review questions in videos that direct student viewing.

While I have listed five digital tools that might be helpful, remember that it is the quality of the content that drives engagement more than the tool. The tool is merely the delivery vehicle. Continuing to curate the best content is one of the most interesting parts of our professional role. This could be my inner education nerd, but I love designing new graduate and undergraduate classes because I get to assemble the most engaging content from a diverse array of experts. I build reading lists of one to two chapters of the best authors and can include videos and podcasts to introduce my students to remarkable content. I have not taught from a textbook in 13 years, and that is remarkably freeing. Content creation means I am reading 30–40 books a year and count-less articles, but that is the gift of being in higher education, as that is part of my job. I realize the tyranny of the urgent—the demands of students who have real, immediate needs—will keep many of you from this type of intellectual indulgence, but there is joy in this autonomy. In the past year, I have built four new courses and while they will get better each subsequent year, this work has been energizing for me as an educator. See Box 4.1 for how to make space for curation.

4.1 Just Teaching Strategy

Curating Content

If we do not have engaging content, then the tools we use do not matter. Here are a few ideas that might help make content creation more helpful.

1) Start with what students need to know and be able to do. For most of us, this means starting with state standards.

2) Identify the curriculum that your school or district has to teach those standards. Review it with a critical eye. What works and what doesn't?

3) Set aside 30 minutes a week to read, listen, or watch for possible materials you could use within the next month. Always be thinking a week or two ahead of the game. If you have more than 30 minutes, great; but 30 minutes lets you explore without going down a time black hole.

4) Based on your 30 minutes, use this filter: What addresses standards *and* gets me excited about what our class can do?

5) Add this to your content and keep track of how it works.

Thinking of yourself as a content curator for at least 30 minutes a week will energize your teaching and build a cycle of continuous improvement.

One final word of encouragement related to content and content curation—be sure that your content is well-organized. I have found tools such as Schoology and Canvas to be invaluable as learning management systems (LMS) for me and my students. I know many educators have also used Google Classroom and SeeSaw to organize their materials, but whatever system you use, be sure that the content is organized and accessible. For me, that means at the beginning of the semester, all the readings, discussion questions, videos, assessments, and rubrics are loaded onto my LMS. This allows both me and my students to relax, have a clear picture of what is expected and what will be learned, and then focus on each other.

Many well-meaning teachers design units using activities from Pinterest, Teachers Pay Teachers, or other resource sites; however, the sites are not organized to create a coherent scope and sequence. For many teachers, Pinterest and Teachers Pay Teachers can become a social media comparison nightmare of who has the cutest anchor chart or the best kindergarten teacher handwriting. In addition to being unstructured, the comparison game can be crushing because these sites can inadvertently place the focus back on the teacher. Whatever we do with content, we must scaffold it for each student to maximize learning (see Box 4.2 and Box 4.3), which is when we move to consolidation.

Analog option: I still prefer hard copy texts for annotation and discussion. When we discuss readings, I prefer to have a good piece of curated text on paper in front of students. This takes eyes off devices and places them squarely on the text.

Technology Tools for Content

- Newsela: https://newsela.com

- Epic: https://www.getepic.com

- CommonLit: https://www.commonlit.org/en

- Pear Deck: https://www.peardeck.com

- EdPuzzle: https://edpuzzle.com

- Schoology: https://www.schoology.com

- Canvas: https://www.canvas.net

- Google Classroom: https://classroom.google.com

- SeeSaw: https://web.seesaw.me

Find live links to each tool online here: https://baylorcsl.org/justschools/tools/

4.2 Just Teaching Strategy

Maximizing Content

1) What is the content that you are most excited to teach?

2) What is the content that students are most excited to learn? Feel free to ask your students if you are not sure.

3) What is the content that you are least excited to teach?

4) What is the content that students are the least excited to learn? Again, ask your students if they are different than my students, who typically make this abundantly clear!

- Based on your answers to these questions, are there differences between what you and your students think?

- What makes the content exciting to you and your students?

- What steals that excitement for the content you are not interested in teaching?

- Since you probably are required to teach the content that is not energizing to your and/or students, what steps can you take to help that content come to life? If you are not able to come up with any answers right now, perhaps you will get some direction from consolidation, collaboration, or creation.

Consolidation

Students need time and opportunity to consolidate what they know. Friendly competition that allows students to compete against themselves and demonstrate improvement is a great way to encourage students to retrieve knowledge that will build neural pathways that will solidify their ability to apply that knowledge to new learning experiences. Consolidation is necessary for inquiry-based learning to be effective (Kirschner et al., 2006). If we move too quickly to more open-ended projects without a solid foundation of skills and knowledge, students end up floundering in pooled ignorance.

In Chapter 2, we explored some basic principles for games, but all review does not have to be in game form. Anything that allows a student to retrieve and organize their thoughts is a way to facilitate consolidation. Creating graphic organizers, visually representing a concept, teaching the concept to a friend, writing about how a student

learned a concept, or a short hallway conversation can result in consolidation for a student.

Consolidation does not require digital technology; however, there are
amazing free tools available for us to use. Here are a few, and some of
them probably do not need an introduction:

- Kahoot!: I love the Kahoot! music and the energy that builds in a
  classroom when I have built an engaging game. There are many
  options for how to play, but the benefit of Kahoot! is that there is an
  opportunity for a shared experience as tension builds and everyone
  can answer. While there is definitely a podium for the top three
  finishers, everyone can review ideas they have learned through a
  good game of Kahoot!

- Gimkit: Created by a high school student who thought he could
  improve upon Kahoot!, Gimkit allows teachers to create question
  sets that students can answer repeatedly while competing against
  each other, which is great for surface learning and review. Because
  Gimkit allows for repetition of answers and has a variety of ways for
  students to earn points, students remain engaged as they work at
  their own pace.

- Quizlet: Because these quizzes can be created by teachers and
  students and then made available to others, there is a remarkable
  repository of reviews on almost any subject. While we probably
  need to check them to ensure the veracity of the answers, Quizlet is
  a nearly endless resource for review content.

- Nearpod: With many options for reviewing material, Nearpod is
  another great tool for consolidation through review. Additionally,
  Nearpod also owns Flocabulary, which is a library of songs, videos,
  and learning activities that act as earworms with their catchy lyrics
  and music. Flocabulary is great for introducing or reviewing key
  concepts and vocabulary.

Analog option: Using a putting surface, basketball hoop, football
player cut out, and a rubber-band cannon, we played "The Olympics"
at the end of each middle school unit. Teams would have to answer
four consecutive review questions that I asked everyone. When a team
thought they knew all the answers, they would raise their hands and
attempt to answer. If they got them all right, they could pick someone
to compete in one of our events for additional points. This was always
a class favorite and required no digital technology.

Technology Tools for Consolidation

- Kahoot!: https://kahoot.com
- Gimkit: https://www.gimkit.com
- Quizlet: https://quizlet.com
- Nearpod: https://nearpod.com
- Flocabulary: https://www.flocabulary.com

Find live links to each tool in the online companion website.

4.3 Just Teaching Strategy

Cultivating Consolidation

1) Where have you built in opportunities for students to consolidate learning gains?

2) Which of those opportunities do you enjoy facilitating?

3) Which of those opportunities do students enjoy?

4) Where do you see a need for students to consolidate learning gains?

Once you have answered these four questions, consider the tools in this section or other tools that you or your colleagues might have that could facilitate opportunities for retrieval practice. Are there ways that students could help you create more opportunities for consolidation? Again, feel free to ask them!

Collaboration

Collaboration does not necessarily occur when a group project is assigned; and collaboration is different than cheating, which seems to be on the rise (Newton, 2020). These are two important stipulations. In classrooms where meaningful collaboration is occurring, groups of students (with the support of teachers) are developing better work because they are working together. Clear parameters, roles, and criteria for success go a long way toward deepening learning through collaboration (see the example of the Paideia seminar highlighted in Chapter 3).

We can use a wide range of tools for collaboration, and many are available through places such as the National School Reform Faculty (NSRF),

EL Education, or something like an after-action review that helps teams learn from their experiences (Herrmann, 2018). These can be used in person or in a virtual environment and require very little (if any) technology.

However, online tools have proliferated over the last several years for all different economic sectors. In 2021, the software market was over $11 billion and will be over $27 billion by 2028 (Grand View Research, 2021). Not only is this evidence that tools are increasingly available, but skills derived from working with these tools will also be increasingly in demand by employers. I will mention a few here that are representative of some of the types of tools that are available. As soon as these are printed on paper, the individual tools date themselves and are on their way to being replaced by other tools. The tools are not particularly important, but the skills and collaboration they can develop are what matter most and are the reason for their inclusion here.

- For synchronous or asynchronous collaboration on a virtual whiteboard, Mural (see Figure 4.2) and Google's Jamboard are valuable tools. They allow students to organize ideas and move them around on various boards in ways that allow them to capture and organize group thinking. In *The Extended Mind* (2021), Annie Murphy Paul contends that we expand our ability for thinking by getting some of our thoughts out on whiteboards; we free up mental space for additional thought.

FIGURE 4.2   Screen Capture from Mural's Website

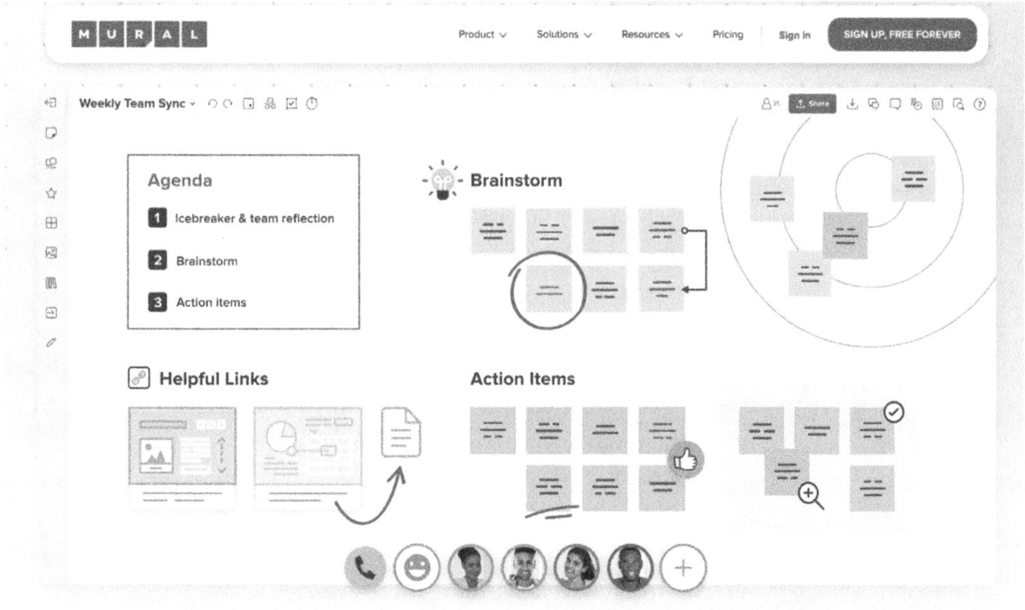

- Parlay is a platform that allows teachers to lead and assess student discussions (see Figure 4.3). The platform captures contributions from individuals and tracks the course of the discussion in the same way that a good Paideia seminar facilitator does on paper. Students can participate in person or remotely, and Parlay captures useful data that teachers can use for assessment and feedback.

FIGURE 4.3   Screen Capture from Parlay That Shows Discussion Data

5. Reflect on engagement as class.

Review class-wide engagement analytics and model submissions as a group. Guiding questions are provided to encourage deeper reflection.

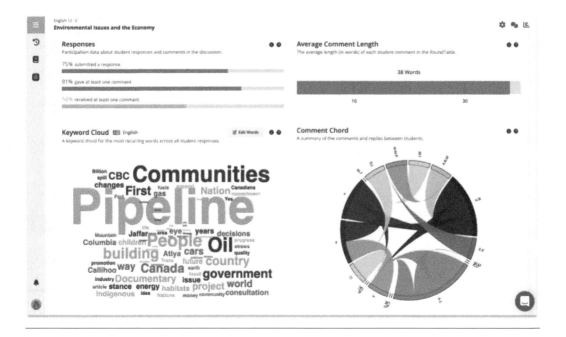

- Mentimeter is my favorite tool of the past three years for immediate feedback and collaboration, especially with large groups. There are similar tools, but Mentimeter is free for presentations that do not use more than three slides and allows students to give feedback in the form of ratings, scales, multiple-choice answers, word clouds, and free response. The results are immediate and show measures of central tendency with the mean and distribution of responses (see Figure 4.4). By capturing everyone's responses remotely, we can engage in more meaningful discussion based on participants' experiences and expertise in a way that allows each individual to inform the collective wisdom of the group.

Technology Tools for Collaboration

- Mural: https://www.mural.com

- Jamboard: https://jamboard.google.com

- Parlay: https://parlayideas.com

- Mentimeter: https://www.mentimeter.com

Find live links to each tool in the online companion website.

FIGURE 4.4   Screen Capture from Mentimeter from a Professional Learning Session

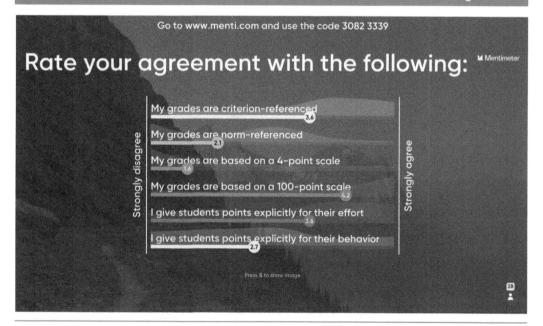

"Burstiness" and Best Principles for Collaboration

Whether we collaborate digitally or analog, we want what psychologists call "burstiness." Burstiness happens when we experience many creative bursts in a collaborative session. Adam Grant, an organizational psychologist, explored this with Trevor Noah, the host of *The Daily Show*, on his podcast (Grant, 2018). According to Grant, burstiness is more likely to happen when people feel safe to take risks and represent diverse perspectives and the

(Continued)

(Continued)

collaboration has structure. The structure makes it possible to share and challenge ideas that feed other ideas that converge and support creativity. To facilitate divergent thinking, we need to do the following:

1) Alternate between group collaboration and individual thinking time to maximize collective problem-solving, as researchers have found that there are ideal rhythms for this collaboration within groups (Bernstein et al., 2019).

2) Elevate the voices of quiet people because they have good ideas (Cain, 2012).

3) Good pitches do not always mean the idea is good. In fact, the definition of a good pitch is selling someone else on an idea that is not good. Therefore, we should always have people pitch others' ideas. This builds collective efficacy and could pair a person who is good at pitching ideas with someone who has a good idea.

4) Middle managers (think school administrators) are typically risk averse. They are risk averse because most have been elevated to their positions because they have made their supervisors look good by building on the vision of others. Therefore, we must help middle managers see the risk of the status quo. When we collaboratively propose new ideas, we have to make clear that *no change* does not equal *no risk*. As teachers, we need to be sure to listen to students from this paradigm as well (Grant, 2016).

Analog option: One of my favorite things to do with my intermediate and middle school students was to create simulations. We survived many ancient civilizations by creating collaborative simulations in which they had to work together against common enemies. Creating clear roles for debates or role-playing games is a lot of fun, is memorable, and brings concepts to life for students. Designing these with students helped improve many of my low-tech simulations (see Box 4.4 to determine how well you cultivate collaboration).

4.4 Just Teaching Strategy

Deepening Collaboration

Based on what you have read and the tools mentioned above, answer the following:

1) On a scale of 0–10, how strong is the collaboration in your classroom? (0 = "We never collaborate because I have all of the best ideas," 10 = "We always get to better ideas and deeper thinking through collaboration"): ____

2) On a scale of 0–10, how strong is the collaboration in your school? (0 = "We never collaborate because the boss has the best ideas," 10 = "We always get to better ideas and deeper thinking through collaboration"): ____

3) On a scale of 0–10, how much burstiness do you observe in classroom collaboration? (0 = "Collaboration is for compliance, not creativity," 10 = "Creative bursts are happening constantly")

4) On a scale of 0–10, how much burstiness do you observe in school collaboration? (0 = "Collaboration is for compliance, not creativity," 10 = "Creative bursts are happening constantly")

What areas do you need to improve around collaboration if we know that collaboration improves with structure, diverse perspectives, and safety?

Creation

Content, consolidation, and collaboration should feed student creation. As students make meaning of the concepts, they should be taking those requisite skills and knowledge to create new work that is meaningful to them. If teaching and learning could function as an apprenticeship in which the teacher imparts skills that the student uses to create something new, receives feedback, refines, and tries again, then schools would explode with creativity, stretching, and growth. Teachers have been doing this for decades without digital technology in the form of papers, projects, presentations, and lab work. The biggest barrier to this kind of work is time. Giving each student the opportunity to create, receive feedback, and refine takes time.

Thankfully, we live in an era where we have many tools that allow students to create and that allow us to give them feedback efficiently and effectively. Again, I will describe a few that are representative but certainly are not comprehensive.

- These first three platforms are great for digital content creation as they are easy to use and offer polished products. Canva allows students to use templates and drag-and-drop images that can create a finished look to their work. Students can collaborate on the Canva platform and create graphics that work well across devices. Similarly, Piktochart facilitates visual storytelling through infographics and presentations that are easy to use and enhance students' ability to communicate visually. Padlet allows students to work together on visual representations that can take the form of a wall, canvas, shelf, stream, grid, timeline, or map. Students can graphically represent disparate and similar ideas relatively simply.

- These next three tools are particularly useful when remote learning is necessary. For example, if you are a math teacher who wants to know what students can do and you are unsure if an online test is giving you accurate information due to students' ability to share answers, these next three options could be quite beneficial to you. Screencastify, Formative, and Loom could all be used by instructors doing their best impersonations of Sal Kahn of Kahn Academy as they are all screen-capture tools. If you have not been online with Kahn Academy, you might not know how these tools work, but basically, they capture whatever is happening on screen and pair it with you voicing over what you might be writing or doing on the screen. These tools are especially powerful when we ask students to work on a math problem while explaining what they are doing. We can get a glimpse of their thinking through these screen- and audio-capture tools.

- The final three tools are excellent for students to have flexibility in how they tell their own stories. We are hardwired to connect through narrative and Flipgrid, iMovie, and Apple Clips all provide flexible ways to give students autonomy in how they express themselves. Flipgrid was probably the tool we heard the most about in 2020 and 2021 as teachers used it to allow students to record their own perspectives and share them with others. The ease of use, flexibility, and ability to connect students have made this a go-to tool for many of the educators with whom we work. iMovie has been around for a long time, but with the release of Magic Movie and other upgrades, it has become increasingly easy for students to do their own digital storytelling and content creation. Magic Movie identifies the best parts of video clips and edits those pieces down so that they can be included in movies with different styles. Apple Clips is an even simpler tool for short videos that can include students' "Memojis" that represent them as their own avatars or actual video. With all three tools, as students begin to capture video, we have numerous opportunities to help them refine their work through self-reflection, peer feedback, and criteria for success that can refine their final products, which are probably less important than the process of telling their own stories.

Analog option: Continue to give students the opportunity to give live speeches or presentations so they engage the class. These can be short, but the ability to communicate succinctly with a visual or verbally continues to challenge and stretch students. Certainly, accommodations can be made based on student needs, but giving students a finite period to engage their classmates in-person is a great opportunity to build confidence and communication skills (see Box 4.5 for ways to increase student content creation).

Technology Tools for Creation

- Canva: https://www.canva.com

- Piktochart: https://piktochart.com

- Padlet: https://padlet.com

- Screencastify: https://www.screencastify.com

- Formative: https://www.formative.com

- Loom: https://www.loom.com

- Flipgrid: https://info.flipgrid.com

- iMovie: https://www.apple.com/imovie/

- Clips: https://www.apple.com/clips/

Find live links to each tool in the online companion website.

4.5 Just Teaching Strategy

Student Creation

Consider the following questions to determine how well content, consolidation, and collaboration are resulting in student creation.

1) How well does the content, consolidation, and collaboration in your class support student creation?

2) Is there any particularly strong area? Particularly weak?

3) What is each student creating in your class?

4) What skills and knowledge are observable in what they create?

5) How are they refining what they create?

6) What could your students be doing differently to enhance creation?

These are hard questions. As a professor, I have to ask myself these questions regularly to keep students at the center of my work. When I was teaching in intermediate and middle grades, I would not have always had good answers for questions three through five. Be honest, as just teaching is all about honesty that leads to improvement.

Engagement is the heart of teaching and the lifeblood of learning. Learning cannot happen without engagement. The ultimate goal of that engagement is student creation.

Student creation is the pinnacle of our work with students because the work is not about us. We are the catalysts and multipliers that identify talent, provide tools, set parameters, and provide feedback. Everything we do with content, consolidation, and collaboration should eventually culminate in creation. This is where we will find true joy in teaching—when the teaching is not about us. An engaging learning experience—even something as unappealing to some teachers as the digestive demonstration might be—becomes rich and meaningful when students begin to ask other questions about their own physiology and design investigations. Before we can get to grades, we have to ensure students are engaged. In the next chapter, we will look at various ways to give students opportunities to engage in deep learning that they own.

Just Teaching Tool #4
Digital Tool Belt

Engagement is about far more than tools, but tools are certainly helpful, especially when they are organized and each has a purpose. Think of this tool as more of a tool belt. What are the tools that you use to cultivate the four *C*s of engagement? You will organize these by *C*s and by frequency of use to help keep these top-of-mind.

(Continued)

(Continued)

TOOL #4 | **DIGITAL TOOL BELT**

TOOLS TO FOSTER THE FOUR Cs OF ENGAGEMENT

LIST THE TOOLS THAT YOU USE TO CULTIVATE THE FOUR Cs OF ENGAGEMENT

CONTENT

Tools	Frequency of Use
_____	Often ○ ○ ○ ○ Never
_____	Often ○ ○ ○ ○ Never
_____	Often ○ ○ ○ ○ Never
_____	Often ○ ○ ○ ○ Never
_____	Often ○ ○ ○ ○ Never

CONSOLIDATION

Tools	Frequency of Use
_____	Often ○ ○ ○ ○ Never
_____	Often ○ ○ ○ ○ Never
_____	Often ○ ○ ○ ○ Never
_____	Often ○ ○ ○ ○ Never
_____	Often ○ ○ ○ ○ Never

COLLABORATION

Tools	Frequency of Use
_____	Often ○ ○ ○ ○ Never
_____	Often ○ ○ ○ ○ Never
_____	Often ○ ○ ○ ○ Never
_____	Often ○ ○ ○ ○ Never
_____	Often ○ ○ ○ ○ Never

CREATION

Tools	Frequency of Use
_____	Often ○ ○ ○ ○ Never
_____	Often ○ ○ ○ ○ Never
_____	Often ○ ○ ○ ○ Never
_____	Often ○ ○ ○ ○ Never
_____	Often Never

YOU'VE CREATED A DIGITAL TOOL BELT
TO KEEP YOUR TOOLS TOP-OF-MIND

SCAN THE QR CODE
FOR A FILLABLE PDF

Inviting Before Demanding

5

When students lose track of time, they are fully engaged.

Just Teaching

Chapter 5. "Decomplexified"

- Fun and flow can be a part of deliberate practice.

- We need to fill the space in our classrooms to make more space for our students. We can do that in at least 11 ways:
    - Invite students into learning spaces.
    - Have a device policy.
    - See your class.
    - Move away from students when you call on them.
    - Use silence.
    - Use silence again.
    - Expect engagement.
    - End learned helplessness.
    - Do not give warnings.
    - Redirect calmly, firmly, and quietly.
    - Frame everything positively.

- By asking students to signal not to be called on, we move the burden of engagement.

- We should celebrate quirkiness and growth but not days off.

- Our purpose determines how we use our time and tools.

Losing Track of Time

The bell rang to signal the end of the day, and most of the students did not notice. One student who did notice said, "Does that mean we have to stop working?" Nearly 100 middle school students were working in teams on a Mars rover project. They were building prototypes within design parameters that would allow their vehicles to travel across the surface of Mars. They were so engrossed in the work that they did not notice the passage of time and when the bell reminded them of this reality, they wanted to continue to work through the bell.

A few additional details about this context in upstate New York:

- The eighth-grade team teaches in classroom pods that can expand from 24 to 49 to 96 students.

- They do not have a bell system during the day, allowing for maximum flexibility for cross-disciplinary teaching.

- The team uses inquiry-based teaching across all subject areas and maximizes cross-disciplinary inquiry.

- They were having some student attendance issues prior to the Mars rover project.

- During the unit, attendance on most days was 100%.

When was the last time you remember losing track of time because you were so engrossed in an experience? When was the last time this happened to you as a student in a class? When was the last time this happened to your students in one of your classes?

I regularly lose track of time in class when I am engaging students in discussions or listening in on conversations because I love our content and am fascinated by my students' experiences and perspectives. That is why I use timers in all my classes regularly because my deep interest in what one group of students is saying might be hindering the engagement of other students (class could begin to drag for them). In fact, I am not sure how often my students become so engaged that they lose track of time. I know they have not when I see them glance frequently at their phones or at the clock on the wall.

What We Know: Fun, Flow, and Deliberate Practice

Our work should be fun. When I am teaching, one of my primary goals is to have fun. This sounds self-centered, but I have argued for years that our enjoyment as teachers is a precondition of student learning. Therefore, my fun is a necessary precondition of students having fun. Certainly, there are other ways to engage students than through fun and it is not our job to entertain students, but teaching and learning are certainly a lot better when they are fun!

Fun does not equal easy. The Mars rover project was not fun because it was easy. The project was fun because it was challenging, required social connection, and resulted in rewarding outcomes in a way that made students lose track of time. In her book, *The Power of Fun*, Catherine Price (2021) describes *fun* as the confluence of playfulness, connection, and flow. (See Chapter 2 for more explanation.)

First, as I described in *The Novice Advantage* (Eckert, 2016b), playfulness is one of the advantages of being new to something. Even if we become experienced at something, we can approach each day and each lesson from the perspective of being new. Broadway actors have mastered this art as they look at their performances each night from the perspective of the person who is seeing the play or musical for the first time. This type of approach brings energy and playfulness to something that could become trite.

Second, as we explored in Chapters 2 and 3, connection is necessary for meaningful learning. Connections can come between the learner and new ideas or between learners. As a professor, I know I am most engaged in classes where we are all learning together. My favorite class to teach this past year was an eight-hour Saturday course with aspiring superintendents who were pursuing their doctoral degrees. We connected with ideas differently because of the relationships that formed among the 11 of us and the perspectives and experiences that the students brought to each Saturday. We should all walk away from classes where rich connections were made believing that we learned more from others than they did from us—and this includes us as the teachers and professors.

Third, flow occurs when we are completely absorbed in an activity (Czikszentmihalyi, 1990). On good days, this can occur for me while I am writing. Most of the time, writing is a discipline for me, but sometimes, hours can slip by and I will produce 15–20 pages. Sometimes that is the best writing that I will do for the month. Part of fun is creating experiences where flow is likely. To create those conditions, students must be asked to concentrate and fully engage with an idea, others, or (ideally) both to create something meaningful. As I look back on all my years of teaching, I can point to some moments in which students were in flow. These were the times when the bell rang to mark the end of another 51-minute period and students did not want to stop working on their own writing, reading, project, game, or lab.

One problem with fun and flow is that they do not ensure that improvement is happening. Improvement requires deliberate practice—practice that includes feedback from others with expertise and insights to help us grow (Ericsson et al., 1993). For years, I coached my own children's basketball teams from first through eighth grade. Let me assure you that some of my first-grade basketball practices and games were not deliberate in any way. During one game, I only counted four players on our end of the court. I looked back down to the other end of the court and my missing player—let's call him Justin—was making imaginary snow angels on the floor. He was my player who also liked to hug the player he was supposed to guard on the other team. This is the only time well-meaning affection has been whistled as a foul. Justin was not really getting better at basketball even though he showed up at every game and practice. He certainly had fun, but he probably did not experience flow (as that requires some level of concentration) and he was definitely not achieving deliberate practice. He was not developmentally ready to receive feedback about how to shoot a basketball, dribble, pass, or play defense. He got some exercise and was a great source of joy for players, coaches, and parents.

This did not mean he improved at basketball. This is true for many of us. Even as teachers, if we are not receiving feedback on how we are teaching, we have no idea if we are improving. We will dig into feedback extensively in Chapters 6 and 7, but we briefly explore deliberate practice here because this is how we know that students are really engaged.

What Works in Real Schools: Making Space, Celebration, and Growth

Our greatest joy in teaching should be the growth we see in students. This is not a trite platitude. Vocation "is the place where your deep gladness and the world's deep hunger meet" (Buechner, 1973). As teachers, we get to do meaningful work every day to help our students find their own meaningful work—and not only in the future. Our students can engage in meaningful work that addresses the world's deep hunger every day. Unleashing the creative power of our students on seemingly intractable challenges such as hunger, energy, climate, injustice, and crime can address the world's needs while potentially sparking joy in our students as they find their purpose.

To truly engage students' hearts and minds requires science, skill, planning, and art. In his poem, *Undivided Attention*, Taylor Mali (2002) describes the aspirations of each teacher:

A grand piano wrapped in quilted pads by movers,

tied up with canvas straps—like classical music's

birthday gift to the criminally insane—

is gently nudged without its legs

out an eighth-floor window on 62nd street.

It dangles in April air from the neck of the movers' crane,

Chopin—shiny black lacquer squares

and dirty white crisscross patterns hanging like the second-to-last

note of a concerto played on the edge of the seat,

the edge of tears, the edge of eight stories up going over—

it's a piano being pushed out of a window

and lowered down onto a flatbed truck!—and

I'm trying to teach math in the building across the street.

Who can teach when there are such lessons to be learned?

All the greatest common factors are delivered by

long-necked cranes and flatbed trucks

or come through everything, even air.

Like snow.

See, snow falls for the first time every year, and every year

my students rush to the window

as if snow were more interesting than math,

which, of course, it is.

So please.

Let me teach like a Steinway,

spinning slowly in April air,

so almost—falling, so hinderingly

dangling from the neck of the movers' crane.

So on the edge of losing everything.

Let me teach like the first snow, falling.

Fill Space to Make More Space

This kind of teaching requires us to fill the classroom to make more space for students. I wrote about several of these in significantly more detail in *The Novice Advantage* (Eckert, 2016b), but I will provide a few easy strategies for filling the classroom effectively. Here are 11 easy ways to fill the space and engage each student in ways that foster safety and purpose:

1) **Have a device policy.** For smart phones, smart watches, and whatever devices come next, our attention is what technology companies are selling to advertisers. That means they are doing everything they can to keep our eyes on devices. My college students struggle to manage their devices so they can fully engage in class, and I know they have at least slightly more impulse control than a fourth grader. These devices capture attention with notifications, Pavlovian rewards, and 12-second video clips that are going to win when competing with learning experiences designed to build cognitive endurance. Our best option as educators is to create class (and preferably schoolwide) policies on devices. Phone pockets where students can turn in phones when they enter class and pick them up when they leave are one option. Requiring phones to stay in lockers or backpacks is another. Perhaps you are interesting enough to maintain student attention versus a smart phone, but tech companies are betting billions of dollars that nothing is more engaging than their content.

2) **Frame everything positively.** When giving directions or feedback, tell students what you want to see. Focus on what quality thinking, work, and collaboration will look and sound like and describe that. Here is an example: "For the next 10 minutes, your teams will answer this prompt. Your team leader will ensure that everyone contributes at least two comments. Set the orange cone on your desk if you need some assistance from me or one of our class facilitators."

3) **See your class.** Even when talking to small groups, we can position ourselves so that we are facing the class while speaking to the small group. If students are working on tablets or computers, we need to bc able to move around the room to see screens if we do not have screen management software.

4) **Move away from students when you call on them.** This is interpersonally counterintuitive as we typically communicate immediacy by moving toward a speaker, but when a student is speaking as part of a whole class discussion, we want to include everyone in that discussion. By moving away, the students have to project their voices, and this allows the entire class to engage in the interaction.

5) **Use silence.** When I first started teaching, silence in the classroom was a signal to me that nothing was happening and that students were not engaged. Now I welcome silence and create space for productive silence. We have known for over 50 years that increasing the time we wait after asking a question from 1 second to 3 seconds makes a tremendous difference for student engagement (see boxed text below). This does not slow the pace of class significantly, but it gives more students time to process and engage. If you are not good at wait time, moving from 1 to 3 seconds will seem like a long time.

When We Increase Wait Time from One to Three Seconds

- Student responses become 300%–700% longer

- The number of appropriate but unsolicited responses increases

- Failure of students to respond decreases

- Students who are typically less engaged contribute more

- Speculative and predictive thinking can increase by as much as 600%

- Students respond and react more to each other

This is particularly fascinating because this research has been around since at least 1969 (Baysen et al., 2020; Rowe, 1969, 1972, 1986)! In general, slowing down and making space for thinking would benefit all of us.

6) **Use silence again.** After I improved at wait time after asking a question, I realized that I also needed to get better at waiting after an answer is given. When students answer questions, I want to immediately give them feedback, both verbal and nonverbal. I nod my head, smile, use hand gestures, and immediately begin to build on what they are saying. This is not necessarily bad, but this kind of response makes me the de facto judge of whether the response is right or not. If I wait to respond, others listen to the initial student response and evaluate whether or not they agree or if the answer is complete. They are more likely to extend the thinking or offer more perspectives if I wait.

7) **Expect engagement.** This is a simple shift in thinking. There is no opting out of open-ended discussions. Even if answers are not fully formed, we need to communicate to students that they are expected to engage. If we create an environment where it is OK to be wrong or only partially right, we create conditions where 100% participation is possible.

8) **End learned helplessness.** Learned helplessness results from a perception that consequences are random. This can occur when no matter what a student does, they receive positive feedback and assume that their name is all that is really needed on an assignment. More commonly, learned helplessness occurs after years of failure and feeling like no matter what students do, they will not be successful. We can eliminate learned helplessness by giving specific, concrete, and observable criteria for success (more to come in Chapters 6 and 7).

9) **Do not give warnings.** We need to set clear, observable expectations with students and then hold each other accountable for meeting those expectations. If the expectations for work or behavior are not met, we need to move to agreed-upon consequences. The consequences do not have to be immediately severe and, certainly, grace is always possible. For example, if students did not bring a pencil to class, they could borrow one but had to leave a shoe. This way, they received what they needed, they would not leave without the shoe, and they returned the pencil. Constantly giving students warnings or threatening them with what might happen communicates low expectations and creates confusion. Clear expectations and accountability bring clarity and agency.

10) **Redirect calmly, firmly, and quietly.** Doug Lemov (2021) refers to this as the least invasive intervention. Expert teachers conduct classroom management in almost invisible ways. They

focus on prevention rather than reaction wherever possible and adapt approaches for different students (Stahnke & Blömeke, 2021). The key is always to be firm and calm and to emphasize actions you can see. Instead of asking for attention, ask for eyes. Instead of asking a student to stop kicking another student's desk, tell them to put their feet on the floor. See the following boxed text for more ways to redirect off-task behavior.

Here is a possible sequential order to the least invasive intervention:

- Nonverbal intervention: Make eye contact, shake head, move toward the student.

- Positive group correction: "I like how Dante is taking notes."

- Anonymous individual correction: "Three people need to give their attention to the speaker."

- Private individual correction: Approach the student during a moment when students are working and quietly let them know the behavior you expect to see.

- Lightning-quick public correction: "The cell membrane contains— Sarah, eyes on me—cytoplasm."

- Consequence: "Ben, you have 10 minutes of dissection tray clean up at the beginning of lunch."

We want to keep learning at the center of everything we are doing. The less we interrupt with redirection the better. However, when students disrupt their own learning and the learning of others, a natural consequence is something that improves the learning community. As a science teacher, I always offered work that students could do to help prepare for the next lab or clean up the previous one to restore them to our learning community in a way that was just and fair.

---

11) **Invite students into learning spaces.** Before entering our science lab, I gave students a handshake, made eye contact, and greeted them. Depending on the state of public health, this might have to shift to a contactless greeting, but inviting students into the space each day lets them know that today is a new day and they are welcome. Research shows that this simple greeting significantly improves students' academic engagement and reduces disruptive behavior (Cook, Fiat et al., 2018). With college students, that means I get to class at least 10 minutes early and have conversations with whoever is there about how they are doing so that when we get to class time, they know they are welcome and I have a better sense of how they are doing.

These simple techniques make more space for students. They expand the classroom to ensure that each student is seen, heard, and known. (See the box and Figure 5.1 below for more information.)

5.1 Just Teaching Strategy

Filling the Room to Make More Space

Consider the ten techniques. Put a check in the column of those that you use well. If you do not agree with the technique (which is always an option as not everything works well or fits with our own teaching philosophies), place a check in that column. If you think you could use the technique more frequently or effectively, make a note in the final column of how you might do this.

FIGURE 5.1

TECHNIQUES	USE WELL	DO NOT USE	USE MORE EFFECTIVELY
Invite students into learning spaces.			
See your class.			
Move away from students when you call on them.			
Use silence.			
Use silence again.			
Expect engagement.			
End learned helplessness.			
Do not give warnings.			
Re-direct calmly, firmly, and quietly.			
Frame everything positively.			

Please share with a colleague so that you can encourage each other as you refine how you make space for each student.

Signal *Not* to Be Called On

One of the most effective techniques I have ever used for including each student is requiring students to signal so that I do not call on them. I have used this with elementary through college students, and the technique completely moves the burden of participation to the student. As a teacher, I have an almost Pavlovian response to seeing a hand raised. If a hand goes up, I want to call on the student. One solution is cold calling—randomly selecting any student to answer a question. However, cold calling can create unnecessary anxiety for some conscientious students, so we need to reserve that for particular classroom experiences such as rapid-fire review questions that are accessible to all students. To alleviate this anxiety and engage each student, I ask students to give me a signal to let me know not to call on them. The signal is simple, just make eye contact and smile at me. If they do this, I assume that they do not want to be called on at that time. Everything else means they want to be called on (e.g., head scratching, nose picking, staring off into space, rubbing a chin, talking to a friend—see Box 5.2 for more detail). This helps in four ways:

1) This process slows me down and increases wait time. While I am scanning the room looking for signals, I am making eye contact and giving students time to process.

2) This makes calling on a student who might not be paying attention nonpunitive. I can reengage them based on our agreed-upon signaling rules without having to chastise them for off-task behavior.

3) I am in a much happier mood because my mirror neurons are getting a lot of smiling faces when I am teaching a tough lesson.

4) When being observed by others when I am teaching a tough lesson or not teaching very well, it looks like I have a lot of happy, engaged students.

5.2 Just Teaching Strategy

Signals

1) How do students let you know that they need something or have a contribution to make?

2) Does this help build in strategic wait time to open the space for more responses?

(Continued)

> (Continued)
>
> 3) Have you ever tried to have students signal you to not be called on?
>
> 4) Would you ever try having students signal you to not be called on?
>
> 5) What are some creative ways you might open space for more students to contribute in effective ways? Please share them with me, as I am always open to more ideas and borrowed this idea of signaling to not be called on from an award-winning high school science teacher. (Contact info: jon_eckert@baylor.edu | Twitter @eckertjon | www.jonathaneckert.org)

Celebrate Quirkiness, Not Days Off

The older I get, the more convinced I am that everyone is a little quirky. That probably means that I am quirky and getting even quirkier. As long as the quirkiness is not antisocial, this is something that we need to lean into and model for our students. This goes for elementary through graduate students. Why? Students prefer authentic, passionate teachers and find them more approachable (Johnson & LaBelle, 2017). And quirky is way more interesting than normal. I am also increasingly convinced that there is no normal, so let's celebrate the quirkiness of others by being willing to embrace our own idiosyncrasies. Our students certainly have plenty of them.

In one parent–teacher conference, a teacher shared that her fifth-grade student would sometimes bleat like a goat to be called on. As the parent in the parent–teacher conference, I was somewhat appalled to learn that the fifth-grade child was my daughter. The teacher took it all in stride and had redirected my goat-child to focus her creative love for animals in other directions without crushing her spirit. While I am certainly not advocating for making animal noises to be called on, I am an advocate of finding ways to bring ourselves into the classroom.

One of the things that elevated the identity of several students was the use of nicknames. By the time students had been with me for a year, they all had a nickname that we used in class. For one year, I taught fourth grade and then moved up to fifth grade the following year. I wanted to loop with my students—the process of taking your entire class with you to the following grade—but that was not possible with the way our school was structured. Therefore, I was only able to keep seven of my students. One of those seven students was something of a legend in our school. In kindergarten, when he was asked to pick something up for his teacher, he responded, "What's the matter with you? Your legs broke?" He was quite small for his age, which only fed his Napoleonic complex, and he had alienated most of the class in kindergarten through third grade. To feed his need to be larger than life and in charge of something, we nicknamed him "The Bull" (especially popular given our school's proximity to the Chicago Bulls) and put him in charge of caring for our class bunny, Priscilla. The Bull took unbelievable care of Priscilla, who functioned in some ways as our class mascot, and he used his take-charge attitude for good . . . most of the time. Eventually, he built Priscilla an amazing indoor/outdoor hutch at his home and took her home, where she lived out a very happy retirement from class pet responsibilities at the end of our second year together.

The Bull was quirky, but when given an identity and particular role in our class, he thrived. He was far more engaged in learning, and I was better able to connect with him; he and his mom even invited me over to have dinner with the family, including his grandparents. The four of them lived under the same roof. I quickly realized where the kindergarten version of The Bull picked up the phrase, "What's wrong with you? Your legs broke?" as that was the kind of banter that flew around a home of Chicagoans where a little boy lived with three housemates whose average age was 57.

One last note—if we want students to be engaged, then we have to be engaged as well. We need to celebrate the individuals in our classes, but only celebrating times when we don't come to school sends the wrong message to students. We should never have countdowns to holidays in our rooms or celebrate snow days. Even if we feel some internal joy about the blessed reprieve of an unexpected day off due to snow or a much-hoped-for break, let's avoid celebrating this with our students. Instead, let's communicate that every minute with them is precious. Think back to being a student and the teacher from whom you learned the most. Didn't they communicate that every moment was important and that they would rather be with you than anywhere else? We owe it to our students to be fully engaged and protective of every minute we can spend with them. If we have the margin (this is a big *if*, and we should only do this if we have margin) and can coach, sponsor a team, or find other ways to spend more time with students, then we do that as well.

Try not to let students see us celebrating time away from them. Instead, what if we celebrated students as we neared breaks? From elementary to middle school to graduate classes, the last days of class have always been a celebration of the amazing things our class has done over the year. This is a great time to celebrate quirkiness. In Chapter 2, I wrote about the student quote board we had in our room. We would read and record each of those quotes on video and share them with the class on the final day of school. Here are some of my favorites:

"I eat healthy, so I don't eat at McDonald's. I eat at Sonic."

"I want the grades I don't get."

"I know life is not fair, but why can't it be unfair in my favor."

Whatever we do, we should be celebrating students and learning and not time away from them. (See Box 5.3.)

5.3 Just Teaching Strategy

What Do You Celebrate?

We elevate what we celebrate. This makes what we celebrate pretty important. I am a big fan of celebrating the individuality of students because it is what makes our work infinitely interesting. I also love to celebrate growth and achievement.

1) Think about your classroom celebrations. Do they accurately focus on highlighting what you value?

2) Pick one quirky thing about your classroom or your learners to celebrate. What might that celebration look like? How can you involve students in choosing and planning?

3) Is there a celebration that may be sending the wrong message about your classroom values? How could you eliminate or refocus this?

If you find a lack of alignment between what you celebrate and what you value, begin thinking with your colleagues about how to better celebrate what you, your students, and your community value. This is a great way to have a deep but fun conversation about what it means to teach for justice and to have flourishing students.

Elevate All Forms of Growth

Like many families, in our house outside of Chicago, we had a doorframe that recorded the heights of our family—all five of us plus our dog, Charlie. For ten years, we had marked the growth of our family. When we moved to Texas, we left that door frame and those markers behind. Four months after we left, a friend who was babysitting for the family that had moved into our home sent a picture of the doorframe to our youngest daughter, Grace. When she saw it, she asked if there was any way we could get the doorframe and added, "It is the only thing I want for Christmas." Due to the gracious family now living in our former home, a carpenter was able to remove the doorframe and send it to us.

This is a very human response to growth. We all want to see growth. The doorframe was a physical manifestation of growth that had occurred over 10 years in our home. That piece of wood now occupies a doorframe in our new home, and we continue to record the growth that happens here. As educators, it is our job to help our students document their own growth. For academic growth, this might be in the form of a portfolio that demonstrates how students' skills have increased from the beginning of the year to the end of the year. Growth might look more like a chart that tracks improvement on tests of skills or knowledge over the course of the year. Students might see growth in a project or paper that shows where ideas began and where they ended up. Sometimes we might want to show growth as a classroom community. For me, I have used pictures and videos that demonstrate growth over time. The wall outside of my classroom would be covered in pictures that showed students and their lab work from early in the year through the end of the year, where they were conducting their own scientific investigations through the inquiry projects they designed as teams. By June, pictures covered approximately 20 feet of wall. I wanted students to see how they had grown as scientists each day as they lined up along the wall to enter class with a handshake.

Regardless of the ways you choose to track student growth, be sure that they can see they are growing because of their engagement in the work you are doing together. As a reminder, we cannot intrinsically motivate others, but demonstrating growth over time is one of the most important conditions that makes intrinsic motivation more likely. This can be particularly true for social and emotional growth. We have an innate desire to grow. When we witness that growth, we want more of it, which leads to joy, fulfillment, and learning that extends beyond our classrooms. The more we make learning the reward, the more likely we are to create conditions where intrinsic motivation flourishes (see Box 5.4).

5.4 Just Teaching Strategy

Measuring Growth

On a scale of 0–10, how well do you measure the academic growth of your students? _____

0 = "Students grow?"

10 = "We measure and celebrate academic growth daily."

On a scale of 0–10, how well do you measure the social-emotional growth of your students? _____

0 = "Students grow?"

10 = "We measure and celebrate social-emotional growth daily."

On a scale of 0–10, how well do you measure the growth of your classroom community? _____

0 = "We grow?"

10 = "We measure and celebrate classroom community growth daily."

On a scale of 0–10, how well do your students measure their own academic growth? _____

0 = "Students grow?"

10 = "Student measure and celebrate their academic growth daily."

On a scale of 0–10, how well do your students measure their own social-emotional growth? _____

0 = "Students grow?"

10 = "Student measure and celebrate their social-emotional growth daily."

Based on your responses, where do you or your students need to improve the measurement of academic growth? The classroom community?

How can you celebrate progress on your journey toward measuring growth?

Our Purpose Should Determine Time and Tools

When we reduce the purpose of teaching to its essence, we teach to facilitate growth for each student so they can become all they were created to be. By tracking growth, making learning the reward, finding joy, and celebrating what makes each student unique, we create conditions in which we can all flourish. This is why most of us went into education, so what stops us from doing this? We cannot say time because time is merely a measure of our priorities. If we prioritize something, then we make time for it. If school, district, state, or federal requirements are keeping us from the purpose of teaching and learning, then we need to advocate for change. If we are getting in our own way, we need to stop, start tracking our own growth as educators, and celebrate the progress we are making. The only way to know we are making progress is through feedback, the subject of Chapters 6 and 7.

The feedback we receive from students will direct our time and the tools we use. Never use a tool for the sake of using a tool. Tools are driven by their purpose and should not be used to drive a student's purpose. We see this regularly with education fads that pop up and fade away, leaving experienced educators slightly more jaded and cynical because these tools function as technical solutions to adaptive challenges. For example, one-to-one technology device initiatives have been invaluable as we switch from in-person to remote learning and back again. The laptop computers and tablets served as a tool to provide access to content, consolidation, collaboration, and creation. Those are the values of tools. However, laptops and tablets, when used as replacements for flashcards or worksheets, do little to increase engagement. In fact, they can be endless sources of distraction from our intended learning outcomes without appropriate filters and directions. In some cases, a pencil and a piece of paper might be the best tool to engage students. One of our primary jobs as professionals is to create space for each student to maximally learn and to provide a range of tools that will meet each student's needs.

We will know we are thriving when we start tracking progress instead of time. Just like the eighth graders who lost track of time working on their Mars rover project, when we start seeing our growth—and more importantly, our students' growth—we are transformed from employees who punch a clock to professionals who help students transform their own lives. We give them the tools to write their own stories. There is no greater calling.

Just Teaching Tool #5
Self & Peer Reflector

For this tool, you will need a colleague. Hopefully, you have someone that you can trust, but remember that vulnerability leads to trust. Take the lead, be vulnerable, and build deeper trust and a better relationship.

TOOL #5 | **SELF & PEER REFLECTOR**

EVALUATE YOUR CLASSROOM TO IMPROVE STUDENT ENGAGEMENT

ANSWER THE QUESTIONS FOR YOURSELF AND DO THE SAME FOR A COLLEAGUE

ON A SCALE OF 0-10, 0=NEVER AND 10=ALWAYS

	YOU	COLLEAGUE
Each student is engaged in class.		
Each student sees the purpose of class.		
Each student finds joy in class.		
Each student grows in class.		
Each student has the space to grow in class.		
Each student's growth is celebrated in class.		
TOTAL A		
I am engaged in our class.		
I see the purpose of our class.		
I find joy in our class.		
I grow in our class.		
I create space for each student to grow in our class.		
I put students before myself when considering how to engage them.		
TOTAL B		
SUBTRACT TOTAL A FROM TOTAL B		

EVALUATE YOURS AND YOUR COLLEAGUE'S RESULTS
ARE THERE DISCREPANCIES? ANY SCORES PARTICULARLY LOW? WHY? WHAT MIGHT NEED TO CHANGE?

SCAN THE QR CODE
FOR A FILLABLE PDF

Part III

Feedback

The next two chapters explore how we can give and receive meaningful feedback. Feedback is the lifeblood of teaching and learning because it is the conversation between teachers and students that helps us all grow. Far from being teaching's necessary evil, feedback is where we see the fruits of our labor.

FEEDBACK, ENGAGEMENT, & WELL-BEING

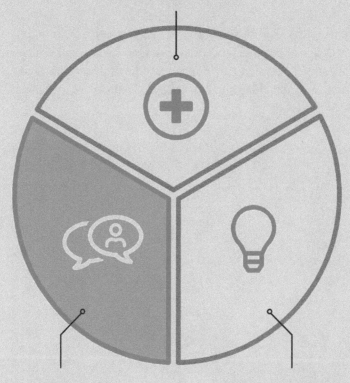

WELL-BEING
PURPOSE-DRIVEN FLOURISHING

FEEDBACK
PURPOSE-DRIVEN
WISDOM FOR GROWTH

ENGAGEMENT
CONTENT, CONSOLIDATION,
COLLABORATION, CREATION

Habits Before Goals

6

Changing habits changes trajectories.

Just Teaching

Chapter 6. "Decomplexified"

- Assessment is more than judgment and evaluation.

- Micro-changes in daily habits that we regularly assess transform lives.

- Deliberate practice, not just practice, leads to growth.

- To live is to grow.

- Eight-step feedback focuses us on students and their work.

- Learning should function like an apprenticeship: Students are regularly receiving feedback, improving, receiving more feedback, and improving again.

- Unlike advice, feedback is about building habits toward a goal. Feedback needs to be specific, timely, and received.

- Cheating robs teachers and students of meaningful feedback and is the enemy of growth.

- We can elevate habits to rituals by regularly giving public feedback on culture-building contributions.

Habits

Educators are special. We get to set new year's resolutions twice a year—in August and January. We have two annual opportunities to set ambitious goals to better ourselves, classrooms, and schools.

Then we reach September and February. The excitement of August and January meet the reality of the tyranny of the urgent and seemingly intractable problems. Our disappointments grow in direct proportion to our passion about our previous goals. We must break these cycles for ourselves and our students. If we want to improve, we must create or change habits before we can set meaningful goals. When these habits are rooted in our identity and not based on self-control, they are more likely to stick. James Clear (2018) calls these *atomic habits*—small changes that lead to significant growth.

Ask teachers what they like least about their jobs, and many will say grading. Instead of dreading this part of the job, what if assessment became part of our identities as teachers through our habits? Here is how this might play out for an educator: Instead of setting a goal of assessing all student work within one week of submission—an ambitious goal, particularly if you are a middle or high school English teacher—identify the habits that might make this possible.

1) Set aside 30 minutes of a planning period or after school every day to review a subset of student work.

2) If you still like to give feedback on paper, set out your pens and stack of papers so that when you get to your 30-minute window, everything is ready. If you give digital feedback, be sure your computer is in a quiet, comfortable space.

3) Remove any distractions from your feedback space. In an analog world, that would be other papers or planning materials for the next day. I was always susceptible to planning the next day's lesson over giving feedback to students on previous learning. By focusing on feedback, students get what they need, and I have whatever time remains to prepare for what is next based on how they are doing. If you provide feedback on your computer, shut down notifications, email, and any tempting web or social media portals.

4) When the 30 minutes is up, stop. There will always be more work that requires feedback. Working too long burns us out for the next day.

By making micro-changes that we apply daily, we begin to change how we and others think of ourselves. If we begin to see ourselves as people who regularly provide meaningful feedback to students in a timely manner, then that becomes part of our identity. Once we identify as these types of educators, habits are easier to maintain. For example, people who are attempting to establish a habit of running daily will be more likely to do this if they identify themselves as runners rather than as people who are trying to run—identity over willpower (Clear, 2018).

Not all habits are good, and we need feedback to let us know which ones to keep, which ones to abandon, and which ones to tweak. Assessment and feedback are the primary tools for developing habits that transform lives. If that sounds odd to you, it is possibly due to a misunderstanding of assessment and feedback. Before reading any further, go to Box 6.1.

6.1 Just Teaching Strategy

Defining Assessment

(1) When you hear the word *assessment*, what words come to mind?

Please list at least three words here:

(2) When students hear the word *assessment*, what words come to their minds?

Please list at least three words here:

(3) Please share your words with others on your team. When you hear the different words listed, why don't we like the word *assessment*?

As human beings, we do not like to be evaluated or judged. Unfortunately, that is how assessment feels to a lot of people and is a reason why many of us do not really like to share new year's goals or resolutions with others. We fear the judgment that will come when we fall short. We fear judgment of the failure even more when we see ourselves as failures and root our identity in our performance. Assessment is a threat to our identity and self-worth.

But it shouldn't be! *Assessment* comes from the Latin root word, *assidere*, which means "to sit beside." This should completely transform the word for us. Instead of evaluation, judgment, or tests, assessment leads to feedback for improvement. Assessment and feedback are linked. Assessment is the conduit through which we give and receive feedback. When sitting beside another, feedback is all about improvement. To give and receive good feedback, we need good assessments. As educators, how can we sit beside our students and give them feedback on a regular basis that informs their habits? How can we invite other educators to sit beside us as we grow in our skills, knowledge, and habits of mind? In this chapter, we will focus on feedback for teachers and students because it is necessary for habit-forming growth. In Chapter 7, we will dig more into assessments.

Grant Wiggins (2012) wrote,

> The term "feedback" is often used to describe all kinds of comments made after the fact, including advice, praise, and evaluation. But none of those are feedback, strictly speaking. Basically, feedback is information about how we are doing in our efforts to reach a goal. (p. 1)

While Wiggins mentions a goal here, feedback is really about the habits we build toward that goal. If our goal is to engage students, we need regular feedback to determine if that is happening, so we regularly scan the room to see if students are nodding off, we ask questions, and we invite others in to give us feedback. In the same way, our students need consistent feedback on their own habits that lead to goals. Feedback is the through line that connects effort and growth to success.

> Feedback is the through line that connects effort and growth to success.

Feedback is not only for students. Katie Kilpatrick, a high school teacher, asks students for feedback at the end of each trimester. She asks, "What is another teacher doing that you wish I would do?" This kind of question allows students to give constructive feedback in a positive way that Katie can filter for what might improve her classroom. Regularly seeking and using feedback from students is a characteristic of effective educators (Kumar et al., 2019). Teachers who invite feedback from colleagues improve significantly based on students' academic achievement (Kraft et al., 2018).

The best way to improve is through deliberate practice (Ericsson et al., 1993) which requires feedback from a more advanced peer or mentor. Someone learning how to play chess is going to improve much more quickly with feedback from a more advanced player than simply trying to muddle through on their own. That is the epitome of assessment, and formative assessment of daily habits is the secret sauce that will lead to the summative assessment of longer-term goals.

What We Know: Feedback Accelerates Growth

One of the most cliché sayings in education is that we seek to grow life-long learners. However, it is a cliché because it is true. We are hard-wired for growth. From the cradle to the grave, we have an innate desire to improve. Watch a baby learning to crawl or a retiree pick up golf, chess, or Wordle.

When we walk into a classroom that is full of life and energy, we see the physical manifestation of growth. When we enter a room drained of life and energy, we see students who are already withering.

Let me illustrate with three classroom visits I conducted within a month. The first two visits were in two different urban contexts, and the third was in a more suburban area.

> Scene 1: I walked into the second-grade classroom. The timer on the board read 7 minutes and 56 seconds. Two students snuck a furtive look at me as I entered the room. One even ventured a shy smile. The teacher sat at her desk, and the students sat in rows with food trays of gray pizza, apples that looked small enough to be crab apples, and milk cartons on their desks. A student started to say, "Hello." The teacher cut him off. "No talking. You know that you all don't eat your lunches if you talk." I looked at the timer on the board, 6 minutes and 42 seconds.

In a little over a minute, I observed a teacher suck the life out of a class-room. Marcia Tate (2016) asserts that we spend the first three years of life teaching kids to walk and talk and the next 15 telling them to sit down and shut up. This is not feedback that leads to growth. If students receive this kind of feedback at lunch, what does class look and sound like?

If assessment means "to sit beside," then it would be unfair for me to judge the entire classroom on that small interaction without first under-standing more of the context. However, wouldn't it be better if several educators came alongside and figured out a better way to eat lunch, teach social skills, and breathe joy into an atmosphere that felt more like prison than second grade?

The second visit was to an early childhood center:

> Scene 2: Students were engaged in creative play and drawing with teachers and paraprofessionals. The room was noisy in a good way, with active learning all around. When one three-year-old student saw us, he came and wrapped our legs in a mini bear hug. His teacher said, "He is the ambassador for our school. He welcomes everyone."

This school did not have any more resources than the previous school and students faced similar challenges, but the environment could not have been more different. Teachers were physically sitting beside students and giving them feedback on how to grow. That feedback fed joy instead of robbing students of it.

These examples are from primary grades, but I can also cite evidence of life-giving classrooms from all levels. Here is one more snapshot: a high school innovation lab that had formerly been a dog food factory.

> Scene 3: We walked into the lab filled with equipment for robotics, electric cars, machines for fabricating tools and parts, and rocketry. Alongside a teacher, students were designing a water system for a village in a developing country in partnership with a nonprofit that was physically building the system. Another student who had received a week of professional training on an advanced piece of machinery with his teacher explained to us how the machine worked. As an aspiring engineer and debate member, he eloquently explained how engaging with the lab had put him on a trajectory to attend Stanford University.

Students were solving real-world problems *alongside* their teachers. As their competence grew, so did their autonomy. This is powerful because autonomy is an essential component of motivation (Deci & Flaste, 1995). The student who explained how the machine worked was one of only two people in the school who knew how to use it, and he was now training others. The work students were doing in the innovation lab functioned as a type of apprenticeship—an essential component to life-giving feedback that develops the habits students need to flourish (Seligman, 2011). Students attempted to solve problems individually and collaboratively, received feedback, improved their efforts, and tried again until they achieved acceptable solutions.

We need more scenes like two and three to develop the kinds of habits students need to be powerful learners. In fact, we need more of these scenes to help us to be powerful learners as educators. Unfortunately, many students find themselves uncertain of how to achieve success on meaningful tasks. Box 6.2 provides an exercise that is an adaptation of the work Jim Nottingham proposes (Nottingham & Nottingham, 2017).

6.2 Just Teaching Strategy

Draw a Classroom

Feel free to do this on your own or with a colleague, a team, or some students.

1) Take two minutes and draw a classroom—any classroom.

2) If you are doing this with others, take 30 seconds to give each other feedback on the drawing. If you have done this on your own, find someone to give you feedback on the drawing. Do not worry if your drawing is never going to end up in a museum, you just need some feedback.

3) Record the feedback you received here:

4) Would the feedback have helped you improve your drawing?

5) "Grade" your drawing based on this rubric*:

20 points for a door

10 points for a teacher's desk

1 point for each student's desk

5 points for a window

30 points for a teacher

1 point for each student

(Continued)

(Continued)

6) How did you do? Is this a good measure for the quality of your classroom drawing? If you did this with others, was the most interesting classroom the highest scoring classroom? Did this "rubric" account for nontraditional classrooms?

7) What if we would have co-constructed the criteria for a successful classroom drawing?

8) How much easier would it have been to give feedback?

9) How much easier would it have been to be successful on the assignment?

(*Note: This is really a checklist, not a rubric. A rubric has to differentiate performance levels; however, many teachers will refer to a checklist like this as a rubric. Keep reading for more on this.)

The assignment in Box 6.2 is not likely an assignment we would ever use. However, teachers put students in this position regularly. Assessment becomes a game of guessing what the teacher wants. Students are less focused on what they are actually learning and are more focused on what will make the teacher happy. If you have ever been in this position as a student, you know how frustrating this can be. We can easily remedy this and ensure that it does not happen in the future. We need to move toward timely feedback on meaningful, authentic assessments.

Eight-Step Feedback

Focusing on quality assessments and meaningful feedback simplifies our work because they take the focus off us as teachers and place that focus squarely on the student. We are no longer performing; instead, we are giving feedback on student performance. The best way to do this is through an eight-step process. While an eight-step process might not seem like simplification, it is simpler because it focuses us on refining high-quality work instead of churning out multiple assignments or keeping the spotlight on us as teachers. Figure 6.1 represents the eight steps that move us beyond merely reporting grades to an apprenticeship. We agree on a goal, the student/apprentice makes an attempt, receives feedback, revises, attempts again, revises, and so on until they reach mastery. Instead of silversmiths, students become historians, mathematicians, editors, and scientists.

FIGURE 6.1 Eight-Step Feedback

This feedback model is derived from Jim Nottingham's seven steps for feedback.

Step 1: Know the Target

The intended goals of the performance task must be clear to the teacher *and* the student. When I first started teaching (and even now when I am teaching a new class), I will put hours into a performance task description and rubric and will be very confident that the goals are clear; however, the most important people who need to be clear on the assignment—the students—are not always as clear as I am. To avoid this, either build the goals together or, when you first introduce the task, have multiple students explain to you what they believe the purpose might be.

Step 2: Develop the First Final Draft

Instead of telling students to submit a rough draft to represent their initial draft, we need to ask for their best effort on this attempt. The more effort and quality they put into their first effort, the deeper the feedback they can receive.

Step 3: Check the Target

Using the criteria for success described in Step 1, students can review their first final drafts. They can do this on their own, with peers, or both. There are two keys to this step: a quality first final draft and clarity on what the students are looking for in the draft. Training students to focus on the identified criteria and helping them to see critical feedback as vital to improvement are important life skills and vital to the process.

Step 4: Improve

Now students have a purpose for the feedback they have received—improving their tasks. Even though most of us do not want to be evaluated or judged, we all have an innate desire to improve. Students can now elevate their work through a second final draft.

Step 5: Teacher Checks the Target

This might seem late, but this is the blessing of this process. When students take the first four steps, the quality of work we receive at this point is significantly higher than it would typically be. At this point, we should be fine-tuning the work based on the criteria for success we agreed upon in Step 1. I will use a rubric to let students know where they stand and provide either voice notes in our learning management system (LMS) or written notes on the assignment or rubric. This has cut my feedback time to students significantly.

Step 6: Improve Again

Students can take our feedback and refine a third final draft. At this point, students are typically proud of the work they have developed and have a strong sense of ownership.

Step 7: Grade

This chapter is titled, "Habits Before Goals," because feedback is more important than grades. That does not mean goals or grades are not important. It simply means that grades are the point at which students know how well they have met the criteria for success. We can report on their success at this point without any sense of guilt. They have now had three opportunities to produce quality work. Hopefully, the grade is a celebration of that work and is closely aligned with the initial criteria.

Step 8: Reflect

Both teachers and students should take a few minutes to reflect on the performance task.

As teachers, we need to ask ourselves the following:

- What went well for students?

- How well did each student meet the criteria for success?

- What do they need to do next?

- What should I change for this performance task in the future?

- How does this performance task inform the next one?

For students, they need to ask themselves the following:

- What can I celebrate about this performance task?

- What did I do exceptionally well?

- What could I have done better?

- How did my work improve?

- What do I understand and what can I do now that I could not do before?

This reflection can be formal or informal, but it is critical to spend some time consolidating the success that was achieved through the process. Obviously, this process takes time, but by devoting time to this work, we focus on what is most important—what students know and can do (see Box 6.3).

6.3 Just Teaching Strategy

Unleash Eight-Step Feedback

Does eight-step feedback feel overwhelming or liberating to you? If it does not feel liberating, why not? Use the following questions to determine what you might be able to apply.

1. How might the quality of your students' work change with eight-step feedback?

2. How might you use time in class differently if eight-step feedback drove your instruction?

3. How might students respond to this approach?

4. Where have you already developed good feedback loops?

5. Are you working harder than your students on feedback?

Based on your responses, reach out to a colleague and figure out how you can make teaching more about students and the work they do through eight-step feedback.

What Works in Real Schools: Consistent Feedback Based on Authentic Work

Feedback is about the habits we build toward that goal. If our goal is to engage students, then we need regular feedback to determine if that is happening; we regularly scan the room to see if students are nodding off, we ask questions, and we invite others to give us feedback. In the same way, our students need consistent feedback on their own habits that lead to goals.

To give effective feedback, the criteria for success need to be clear for teachers and especially for students. The first time I give an assignment at any level, I have an idea in mind of what success will look like. However, I am frequently surprised by the first attempts I get from students because even though I have given them a rubric, my expectations are never as clear as I thought they would be. We cannot overcommunicate the criteria for success. We must be explicit, provide examples, and ensure that we give feedback throughout the work. We cannot GPS them—have them mindlessly following our directions with no idea of the how and why of what they are doing.

When we give feedback, we need to be direct and encourage growth. Teachers who begin their feedback with the phrase, "I'm giving you these comments because I have very high expectations, and I know that you can reach them" found that students were twice as likely to revise their work (Yeager et al., 2014).

This is an essential point. Our focus cannot be on giving feedback. Our focus has to be on how feedback is received. At a Visible Learning Conference in 2018, John Hattie said, "It is not about how much feedback we give. It is about how much feedback is received." The only way to know if feedback has been received is to see if it has been applied. Wiggins (2012) suggests that we need to avoid giving advice—telling people what they need to do—and first give feedback on what we did or didn't do. For example, teachers working on higher levels of student engagement need feedback on how each student is responding. They could get this through various means such as video recordings of the class, student surveys, student work samples, or a peer observation explicitly for student engagement. Before receiving feedback, we need to see what we are doing so that we see a need and context for the feedback. To give effective feedback, we first have to acknowledge three tensions: feedback given vs. feedback received, specificity vs. timeliness, and cheating vs. growth.

> Our focus cannot be on giving feedback. Our focus has to be on how feedback is received.

Feedback Given vs. Feedback Received

One of the saddest things I see in classrooms from elementary school through college is students disregarding deep, meaningful feedback. Stand in a middle school or college hallway after students receive feedback on a final draft of a paper or report. The instructor spent hours annotating and identifying areas of strengths and weakness and assigned a grade. If the feedback came via paper, you will see many students look at the grade, ignore the feedback, and then discard the paper—sometimes into the recycling but sometimes on the nearest available piece of floor. When the feedback comes electronically, sometimes the students see the grade and never return to the carefully annotated comments or audio feedback from the teacher.

This is particularly sad for me because teachers put a great deal of time into meaningful feedback on students' work, and sometimes students receive no benefit from this work done on their behalf. We must teach students how to receive and apply feedback well. To do that, students need reasons to apply the feedback.

Here are a few habits to increase students' ability to receive and apply feedback. Students and teachers should be able to answer five questions when working through an assignment. If they can, they are more likely to improve their work through feedback (Nottingham & Nottingham, 2017).

1) What am I trying to achieve?

2) How much progress have I made so far?

3) What should I do next?

4) WITFM (What's in it for me)?

5) WAGOLL (What's a good one look like)?

If we can help students answer these questions, then we will get much better work from them, which gives us a better opportunity to give them meaningful feedback. Questions four and five are key. As teachers, we need to give students feedback when they still have time to improve their work. If we give students feedback after they have already received their grade, then there is very little reason in their minds to attend to that feedback. Some might push back and say that giving feedback prior to giving the grade will result in grade inflation. However, if our job is to help students achieve at high levels, isn't our job to help students produce the best work possible that meets or exceeds standards? Good feedback asks questions, probes, and demands more detail, but it does not do the work for students.

That is why question five is so important. Giving students exemplars provides clarity. We do not want them simply to replicate that work, but they need a clear vision of what success looks like—a key component of student success (Hattie, 2009). As a teacher, I have always found that it is helpful for me to do the assignment and share my work with students before I ask them to do the same. After the first time I give the assignment, I always ask three to five students if I can keep their work as exemplars for future classes. This does at least two things: By asking to keep theirs as an example, I affirm the quality of their work; and I have a range of exemplars that demonstrate how students can be successful in different ways. By providing these examples and clear expectations, we habituate excellence in our work and in students' work.

Specificity vs. Timeliness

We need habits to make feedback manageable, especially if we are responsible for large numbers of learners. The greatest feedback challenge I have faced is the tension between specificity and timeliness. For the sake of my own survival and the benefit of my students, I have learned to err on the side of timeliness. As a middle school teacher, I was responsible for feedback for approximately 125 students a day. Depending on your context, this might not sound like a heavy load, but for me, giving feedback to 125 students was challenging. We set habits and routines to make feedback timely. Students would submit a lab report and two to three quizzes a week in addition to tests over the course of a semester. For the lab reports, quizzes, and tests, I reduced my focus and sped up feedback—a form of flash feedback (Johnson, 2020). For the lab reports, I focused on the last section of the report in which I always asked the following question: "What concept did you learn in the lab today that connects with what we have been reading and discussing? Provide specific examples and connections." I scored the rest of the lab report for completion, but this question always determined whether students could connect the concrete lab experience to the abstract concepts we were discussing. For quizzes, I would sometimes use tools such as Kahoot!, Gimkit, Nearpod, Quizlet, Plickers, or class response systems that quickly provide feedback to each student as to whether they had done the reading that would prepare them for class. (These and other resources are linked from the online companion website.) Once the game was done, I had my data to import into my gradebook and students had their feedback. For any portion of unit tests that were multiple choice that could be machine graded, I would score those for students immediately before they left class, leaving me only the extended responses that were necessary to assess separately. In other words, to give feedback in a timely manner, choose the most important focus for the assignment instead of belaboring comments on every detail.

By creating these opportunities for flash feedback, I had more time for the deeper feedback that requires greater specificity. As we will explore later in the chapter, by being clear on what type of feedback is required, we can allocate time appropriately. With direction, students can give surface-level feedback to each other or receive it in an automated way, which gives teachers more time to give feedback on performance tasks that require more nuanced attention.

Cheating vs. Growth

Cheating is a critical issue when considering feedback. Feedback can be given, received, timely, specific . . . and completely worthless if it is not an accurate representation of student or teacher work.

In my conversations with them, students at all levels from elementary grades through graduate students report what appears to be an epidemic of cheating. However, many of these students don't see what they're describing to me as cheating; they do not see cheating as an issue. Cheating has become a habit because students are valuing grades or their free time over learning. They see it as the evolution of collaboration. Based on a survey of over 70,000 high school students, 95% reported cheating in some form, 58% admitted plagiarizing, and 64% said they had cheated on a test (McCabe et al., 2012). During the COVID-19 pandemic, a company that tracks cheating on online exams found an increase from 1% to 8% (Newton, 2020). As one administrator told me in reference to the rampant cheating he saw occurring while students were learning virtually, "At least students are learning how to work together." He believed that this was a positive result of students sharing their work on tests or other assessments. Cheating also includes plagiarism in that students are claiming others' work as their own.

Alyssa Carl, a high school math teacher, shared a particularly egregious form of "collaboration." She received screenshots of a mother's Facebook page. The mother had posted her son's math test online to crowdsource answers to the test. In her post, she wrote, "Cannot figure these out. . . . Can anyone put some insight into these? already got some of them done but these I need help" to which a man posted all the answers and then said "I've commented with answers/work on each picture. You might have to massage some of the work to fit into what the teacher wants." When the student submitted the test and got a poor score, the mom emailed and asked how he could have scored so poorly when she even "had a mathematician help on the problems."

Many students, and clearly some parents, believe that cheating is acceptable now. They see the grade as the ultimate goal instead of learning. This is an enormous problem on at least three levels:

1) **Cheating is wrong.** Individuals are claiming work, skill, and knowledge that are not their own. In future work or collaboration, they will only be able to contribute their ignorance to collaboration that will be vacuous if composed of other students who have not acquired requisite expertise either. Once a student begins to cut corners, those practices begin to spiral into cutting even more corners because they form habits. Employers want to know what an employee knows and can do. More importantly, they want to know what they will do when no one is looking. That is integrity.

2) **Cheating erodes trust.** Doctors, engineers, architects, teachers, and pilots who cheated their way through school frighten me. At the hospital, when the mask goes over my face and an anesthetic begins to flow, I want to know that I am going to wake up from a procedure that has been done correctly. We trust a credential to tell us that people have sets of skills and knowledge that will allow us to put our lives in their hands. Cheating robs the credential of any meaning.

3) **Cheating is the enemy of growth.** Effective teachers help students move from where they are to where they need to be with appropriate tools and supports. If teachers cannot identify what students know and can do because they cannot accurately diagnose this through valid assessments, then they cannot help the student grow. More importantly, students have no sense of their own skills and abilities if they cheat. Finally, cheating undervalues honest students' work. The students who did the reading, studied, and took the test without the answer key wonder why they did the work when other students who did not read the book can earn full credit on an assessment because another student took pictures of the answer key and shared it.

If we are going to foster growth in classrooms, we must love students well by letting them know that we truly see them and that we see who they are becoming through our assessments. Cheating makes this impossible for teachers to do. To reduce cheating, as educators, we need to reduce grade anxiety, focus on growth through feedback, and emphasize integrity (see Box 6.4 for more.).

6.4 Just Teaching Strategy

Fight Cheating

Several students have told me, "Teachers just need to tell students that cheating is wrong." Most students can cite some teachers who do not allow cheating, and while the students might express some frustration, there is typically a grudging respect. As educators who care about growth, we need to do everything we can to fight cheating even if we cannot stop it all.

Think through these questions, preferably with a trusted colleague or colleagues. Score them on the following scale:

   0: "Strongly disagree"

  10: "Strongly agree"

    1) Claiming someone else's work as your own is wrong. ____

    2) Cheating is an issue in my classroom. ____

    3) Cheating is an issue in my school. ____

    4) Cheating impedes growth. ____

    5) I am actively fighting cheating/plagiarism in my classroom. ____

    6) My students believe cheating is wrong. ____

Here are a few additional questions to discuss: What tempts you to cheat? Are you more concerned about your grade or learning? When is collaboration and answer sharing useful? When does answer sharing become cheating? When does borrowing ideas become plagiarism? What can you do to delineate these differences for your students?

As teachers, we can certainly model how we collaborate, borrow, and share ideas ethically. For example, giving credit to others for good ideas we use in our classrooms is a great start. Eric Johnson, a middle school social studies teacher, uses songs for memorizing countries for geography class. At the beginning of each unit, he reminds students that the previous teacher wrote these songs and that they continue to use them because they are effective and fun.

Feedback As a Ritual

If we want to combat issues such as cheating, we need to elevate habits that build community through learning. As we explored in Chapter 3, rituals elevate habits. The rituals do not have to be exclusively around feedback for academics. In fact, expanding what we give and receive feedback on allows us to celebrate the whole human beings that we are. Rituals can be fun and meaningful for everyone involved. Rituals can improve the cultures of communities.

Ryan Denham is a high school teacher outside of Dallas and he described what his school is doing to promote the kind of culture that educators and students deserve:

> The largest push is for staff and students to recognize each other in public and meaningful ways. Each day, there is a box in the middle of our campus that students can place "shout-outs" in to read during announcements. Students recognize each other for being good friends or helping each other through a bad day. Teachers highlight entire classes for their effort in activities, and students show they value the work their teachers put in with a thank you. This isn't reserved for Teacher Appreciation Week. It is every day. In addition, we have three life-sized Dwayne "The Rock" Johnson and Rocky Balboa cutouts that float around weekly from teacher to teacher recognizing something they did or accomplished. The positive affirmation that goes to each person makes us feel like we are all working toward that same goal. What might be most telling is that we frame every PLC [professional learning community] assessment, activity, club, and event with one question, "Is this best for kids?"

This trajectory-changing public feedback has become a ritual that elevates the habit of looking for the good all around us. The result is authentic praise from peers that builds culture in meaningful ways that transform individuals and schools. Much of this chapter has been on academic feedback, which is a primary function of what we do as educators, but we cannot lose sight of the fact that we care about more than mere academic progress.

Just Teaching Tool #6
Authentic Assessment Designer

Before diving into the assessment designer, answer these questions:

- How does assessment inform your feedback and instruction?

- How can a teacher build authentic, meaningful feedback into every unit?

- How can you get kids involved in feedback to peers in a way that's constructive?

- How can you get feedback from students that will make you a better teacher and learner?

Now dive into the nuts and bolts of building an authentic assessment that will generate meaningful feedback!

(Continued)

(Continued)

TOOL #6 | **AUTHENTIC ASSESSMENT DESIGNER**

CREATE A TOOL FOR ONGOING COURSE IMPROVEMENT

ANSWER THE FOLLOWING QUESTIONS WITH A CO-TEACHER OR CO-PLANNER

(1) **Pick one unit that you know could be more engaging** or that students could demonstrate deeper knowledge or skills.

(2) **Identify what you know about what students know** and can do based on the way you currently assess their learning in this unit.

(3) **What don't you know about their knowledge and skills** that you would like to know?

(4) **What does someone in the field or discipline** (e.g., a mathematician, chemist, writer, historian, editor, or engineer) **need to know or do in the unit?**

(5) **What is an assessment that you would enjoy giving feedback on and grading?**

(6) **How would that assessment align** with any formative assessments in the unit?

(7) **Write out a description** of the assessment.

(8) **Take the assessment** yourself.

(9) **Did you enjoy doing the assessment?** If not, pick something else.

(10) At the end of chapter 7, **you will build a rubric for this assessment.**

TEACH, ASSESS, IMPROVE, REPEAT

SCAN THE QR CODE
FOR A FILLABLE PDF

Feedback Before Grades

7

Feedback is so much more than the grade.

Just Teaching

Chapter 7. "Decomplexified"

- We need to create or use valid, reliable, and timely assessments.
  - We should always give diagnostic assessments well in advance of a unit so we can plan accordingly.
  - Formative assessments are for learning and constitute most of the work we do as teachers.
  - Summative assessments are rare, should be rigorous, and are celebrations of what students have learned.

- Assessment is a continuum:
  - informal checks
  - observation and dialogue
  - tests and quizzes
  - academic prompts
  - performance tasks

- Single-point, holistic, and analytic rubrics allow us to give efficient, equitable, just feedback to each student.

Sitting Beside

How are teachers graded? In Tennessee, we were evaluated every year if we taught Grades 3–8 in English language arts, math, science, or social studies. My students' average improvement from the previous year's exam exceeded the state average by 300% with over a quarter of them scoring better than 99% of the rest of the students in the state (Eckert & Dabrowski, 2010). Our class earned our state-assigned annual valued-added score of *A*. Does this mean that I received good feedback before I received my grade? Did that mean that the grade was connected to the feedback? Other than a few principal walkthroughs and feedback I generated on my own classroom assessments, the feedback was not really connected at all.

When students hear the word *assessment*, they think *grade*. In fact, when I have surveyed students about synonyms for *assessment*, the two most common words they use are *test* and *grade*.

Does it matter that students immediately think of grades and tests when they hear assessment? Why do we need to focus on feedback before grades?

As I wrote in Chapter 6, we need to help students see that assessment really is about sitting beside others so that we can grow and improve together. We need to fight learned helplessness. When we disconnect our efforts from our results, learned helplessness ensues. Even as early as the primary grades, I have seen students who have already disconnected their work from their results. They have bought into the lie that working hard and struggling is a sign of weakness. They believe that intelligence is a trait, not something that develops through struggle. The grade that comes at the end should aid reflection on the growth that has occurred and the growth that the future will require. As teachers, we need quality assessments to provide feedback that supports our learning and student learning.

What We Know: Assessment 101

To give effective feedback, we need a solid range of reliable, valid assessments. Remember, a valid test is one that measures what it claims to measure. A reliable test is one that consistently provides results in a pattern we can trust. (See Figure 7.1, which is a classic graphic representation of validity and reliability.) To determine if our assessments are reliable, we need to ask two questions:

1) Can we trust the pattern that we see?

2) How can we give students multiple assessments to identify a pattern?

By giving students multiple opportunities to demonstrate skills and knowledge, we can identify patterns that help us determine if assessments are reliable. For example, if a student repeatedly demonstrates 90% mastery on formative assessments throughout the unit, we should expect similar performance on the summative assessment.

To determine if assessments are valid, we can ask two additional questions:

1) Could a student do well without really demonstrating understanding?

2) Could a student perform poorly and still have had significant understanding that they could have shown another way?

Validity and Reliability

Think of the targets below as the reported results of an exam. The closer the scores are to the bullseye, the more valid they are because they are hitting their desired target of accurately measuring students' skills and knowledge.

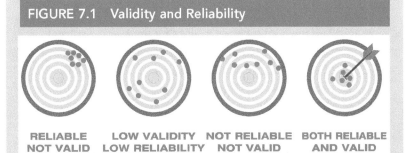

FIGURE 7.1   Validity and Reliability

| RELIABLE NOT VALID | LOW VALIDITY LOW RELIABILITY | NOT RELIABLE NOT VALID | BOTH RELIABLE AND VALID |

Based on these targets, can an assessment be valid and not reliable?

Can an assessment be reliable and not valid?

As you can see, an assessment can provide consistent results while not being a valid measure of what students know and can do. I consistently talk to college professors who proudly announce that the average score on one of their exams is a 66%. They curve the grades (create a distribution of As through Fs with a C equaling a 66% and an A being something like an 80%) because the test is that challenging. This creates at least two problems:

(Continued)

(Continued)

1) The professor might have a reliable test that consistently provides an average score of 66%; however, the test's validity is called into question when they assign a grade based on the performance of other students in the class. If the stated purpose of the exam is to rank student performance—the purpose of a norm-referenced exam—then the assessment achieves this purpose. If the purpose is to let students know that they have effectively understood the pertinent material to move on to more advanced work or classes, then that is unclear because their score is at least equally contingent on the quality of students in the class. For example, a class of premed students taking an introduction to biology course are a more formidable group of peers than communications majors taking the same course to fulfill a general education requirement. A criterion-referenced test would judge student understanding against set criteria regardless of how other students performed—a much better gauge of what students know and can do for future units of study. This assessment would be a more valid measure of what a student knows and can do.

2) Which 34% of the exam was it fine for the average student in the class not to know? In essence, the professor has decided that 34% of the material is not relevant for the average student to understand before moving to the next unit of study. How can this be a valid measure of understanding? The takeaway for the professor should be that students did not have a strong understanding of the assessment and either the test covered material that was not taught or the material was not taught well enough for students to understand. Certainly, learning is a partnership between teacher and student; just as a salesman cannot claim to be effective without sales, we cannot claim to be effective teachers when students do not learn. If the purpose of the exam is to eliminate weaker students from the major or the course, then the exam is more about ranking than instruction.

To be just teachers, we must use assessments that are valid and reliable. For example, consider a common intermediate grade project: At home, create a model of the layers of the Earth with labels, composition of the layers, and relative thickness. We can even create a solid rubric that provides criteria for success. This is probably an invalid, unreliable, and unjust assignment if we are not providing the materials or time in class to complete the assignment. Here's what we really might be assessing: Who has an adult at home willing and able to do this project for/with the student? Whose parents might be willing and able to buy some crafting materials or clay at Hobby Lobby? What happens when we display these projects in the library and students can see whose parents were willing or able to invest time and money in their child's "success"?

Creating valid and reliable assessments is a justice issue. If we are not able to accurately identify what students know and can do, then we are not serving them well. As teachers, if we want to have students demonstrate their knowledge through a project such as this, then the materials and time should be available in the classroom to complete this project. To that end, I see assessment as a constant cycle of improvement. All assessments fall into one of three categories: diagnostic, formative, or summative (see Figure 7.2).

FIGURE 7.2 The Assessment Cycle

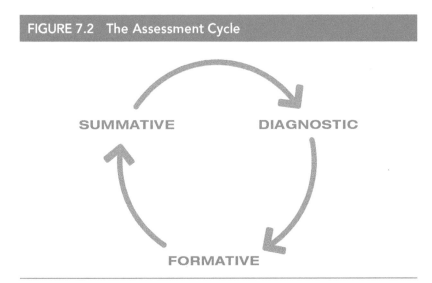

Diagnostic Assessment

The case could be made for only two categories, as diagnostic assessment is really a subcategory of formative assessment. A diagnostic assessment is a formative assessment given before we begin a unit of study.

I separate *diagnostic* or *preassessment* from *formative* assessment because of one hard and fast rule: Never give the assessment on the first day of the unit. So many students become cynical and jaded about preassessments because their performance does not really change anything about their experience with the subsequent unit. If we give the diagnostic assessment on the first day of the unit, that does not give us time to alter the unit for students who have already mastered the requisite skills and knowledge or to adjust for students who are going to need more time. To avoid this trap, I give a diagnostic assessment at the beginning of every school year; I ask students to answer representative questions from our five major areas of study in seventh-grade science. This is the one assessment every year where I hoped students would struggle. Thankfully, I never had a student score above a 56% on the diagnostic assessment, so I knew that students had room for growth in my prescribed curriculum. By giving this diagnostic assessment at the beginning of the year, I was able to do two things:

1) I was able to adjust the lengths of my units based on where particular classes were going to need more or less time.

2) I could identify students who could extend their learning and provide effective peer support to others.

By using these diagnostic data well, I was able to teach and assess everything that state standards required by the end of February. We would review content and skills for one week before the state exam in May, but by using assessment well, I was able to liberate three months of the school year to extend student learning into areas of study that I thought they needed. Diagnostic assessment gave me the freedom to learn and explore with my students.

Diagnostic testing even closer to the beginning of a unit seems to benefit student learning as well. Research shows that pretesting can be an effective form of study. Pretests were better than taking practice tests after learning relevant content. Students who took pretests outperformed students who studied using traditional methods by 49%, and students who used practice tests after studying material improved by 27% on a follow-up test (Pan & Sana, 2021).

Formative Assessment

> Formative assessment is the dialogue between teacher and student that allows each of them to gauge where the other is in the learning process.

Formative assessment is for learning—for both the teacher and the student. Through formative assessment, teachers gauge what students already know and what needs to come next to prepare students for the summative assessment. Formative assessment is to summative assessment as conversation is to relationship. We cannot effectively get to one without the other. Formative assessment is the dialogue between teacher and student that allows each of them to gauge where the other is in the learning process.

Formative assessment leads to formative feedback in which teachers tell a student the truth in love. As teachers, we only serve students well when we provide them with an accurate picture of their progress and provide them with the tools to move forward. This is the primary purpose of formative assessment. Therefore, formative assessment is not about completion. Formative assessment is about accuracy and the development of thought and skills. We know that cheating is a rampant problem that has been exacerbated by distance learning (Newton, 2020). A formative assessment is not helpful if one student copied another student's study guide in preparation for an exam. Read-along sheets that go with homework that requires students to answer questions as they read are likely not effective formative assessments; students view these as another opportunity to show what their more academically talented or diligent friend knows. When we get to meaningful formative feedback, we are building relationships with students around our shared exploration of learning. As teachers, we gain insights into the way their minds work, the way groups interact, and the way we can grow together. When formative assessments provide opportunities for students and teachers to share truth about progress, we are all better for it because we are building trust, skills, and knowledge.

Because students view *collaboration* as taking others' work as their own, we have to be careful about how we formatively assess what each student knows. I am a huge proponent of meaningful collaboration, but for that to occur, each student needs some requisite skills to bring to the collaboration, otherwise group work becomes pooled ignorance. Two to three days a week, my science classes begin with a five-question quiz over the previous night's reading. In my class's structure, the reading always followed the classroom or lab experience so that we could introduce the concept that the reading would reinforce. Based on those five-question quizzes, I had a sense of what was sticking and what was not. The quizzes could be in the form of a Kahoot!, Gimkit, Nearpod, or Quizlet, but most of the time, they were just a half-sheet of paper that we scored in the first five minutes of class. I require students in my college courses to submit their reading responses the night before class so that I can assess what they are thinking as I design class and allow their thinking to inform the session. This practice provides the dual benefit of making my teaching more relevant for them and more interesting for me.

Summative Assessment

The summative assessment has a sense of finality to it because we are making a final judgment on what students know and can do before moving them on to the next topic area or grade. Summative assessments should be celebrations of what students have learned. In essence, we are saying that this is the point at which we are judging learning and are reporting it to others. Most of our assessment is not truly summative. In most of the subject areas we teach, the summative assessment at the end of one unit is a form of diagnostic assessment of the next unit because most curriculum builds on previous learning represented in the iterative assessment cycle.

Helping students understand that learning and assessment are continuous processes is one of the most valuable lessons we can instill. Of course, there will be times when we must evaluate where students are and then send them on to the next level and teacher; however, helping them understand that it is not OK to fail and move on can be powerful. In many classrooms, students can earn a 23% on a summative assessment, get a grade and move on to the next unit with a giant *F* recorded in the gradebook. This means the student did not know 77% of the content on the assessment. How is that OK? Simply put, it is the teacher's job to teach and the student's job to learn. This summative assessment lets us know that one or both of the parties failed to do their jobs. This cannot be acceptable.

My solution for the last 18 years has been to accept nothing below 80% proficiency on key summative assessments. I figure that if a student can demonstrate skills and knowledge at 80% or higher, then we have both done our jobs. On some units when we have done our job well, every college student I have will succeed with a score of 80% or higher. This was rarer with middle school students. If students did not meet the 80% threshold on five key summative assessments throughout the year, they would spend the next few lunch periods with me reviewing material and redoing labs until we determined they were ready to take another version of the summative assessment. With 100 science students, I might have 10–15 students who needed to do this in an average unit. Students would continue with the review and subsequent retakes on summative assessments until they passed the 80% competency threshold. For some, this would take as many as eight attempts, but this effort was entirely worthwhile for at least three reasons:

1) We could continue with students who had demonstrated proficiency in our regular class periods.

2) Students came to believe they could be proficient in science.

3) I had the opportunity to spend more time with students who were struggling, and we built deeper relationships that allowed me to serve them better.

Some would argue that I should have only recorded the final grade that exceeded the 80% threshold, but for those of us who have worked with middle school students, we know what that could mean for some students. They would not put forth a lot of effort on their initial assessment, and I believe there is value in putting forth your best effort on initial assessments. Therefore, I always averaged their assessment scores to give them their final grade. So if a student scored a 40%, 60%, and an 80%, their recorded grade would be a 60% in the gradebook. We will discuss the relationship between feedback, assessment, grades, and issues with the 100-point scale later in this chapter, but for now, we need to start thinking of summative assessments as opportunities to sit beside students to give them the tools they need to be successful. By the time my science students took the state assessment, they knew they were going to be successful. Because of our ability to learn from diagnostic, formative, and summative assessment, we were able to master all our required knowledge and skills by February, which left the rest of the year to explore other areas of science that we found beneficial. Except for a week-long review prior to the state test, we engaged with scientific questions that we chose to explore in labs and through research.

> Because of our ability to learn from diagnostic, formative, and summative assessments, we were able to master all our required knowledge and skills by February, which left the rest of the year to explore other areas of science that we found beneficial.

What Works in Real Schools: Assessment as a Continuum

Diagnostic, formative, and summative assessments take the form of different tools on a continuum (refer again to Figure 7.2). Although this continuum moves from informal to formal assessment and from less time-consuming to more time-consuming, all the data these assessments generate are valuable. We can use any of these types of assessment as diagnostic, formative, or summative as long as we are clear on their purpose.

Look at Figure 7.3. As teachers, we start on the left and move toward the right. As we move from left to right, the assessments are increasingly insightful, but the time required also increases (see Box 7.1).

FIGURE 7.3   Assessment Continuum

INFORMAL CHECKS	OBSERVATIONS & DIALOGUE	TESTS & QUIZZES	ACADEMIC PROMPTS	PERFORMANCE TASKS

INFORMAL & LESS   FORMAL & MORE
TIME-CONSUMING   TIME-CONSUMING

7.1 Just Teaching Strategy

Choose Assessments Wisely

1. Which of these assessment types do you use?
2. Which types are most effective for you?
3. Which would you like to use more?

Informal Checks, Observation, and Dialogue

Good teachers are always informally checking to see that students are tracking with them. Are students engaged with us and with others? How are teams working together? Who is off task? Is someone's head nodding? Is someone else texting under the desk? These are all questions that provide educators with excellent feedback for improvement.

Hannah Kapitaniuk, a second-year teacher, provided a good example of an informal check that identified a nontraditional off-task behavior: "We were going outside as a class, and I noticed two boys were missing. I asked a couple of their friends where they were, and they said, 'They are off hunting turtles.'" These types of informal checks are extremely important and are sometimes overlooked by beginning teachers.

When we are genuinely curious about our students, we have many opportunities for observation and dialogue. In Chapter 5, we discussed ways to engage each student by having them give a signal to not be called on. We can use digital tools that collect feedback as well as Paideia seminar, informal discussions, observations of groups, and conversations before and after class. These processes are the connective tissue of teaching and learning. Creating space for students to show what they can do and are thinking is essential to informal checks, observation, and dialogue. This is a habit that we all need to cultivate.

Tests, Quizzes, and Academic Prompts

Traditional tests and quizzes have a great deal of value for giving students flash feedback and a quick sense of what they know and don't know. Because so many learning management systems or other programs can give immediate feedback on close-ended questions (questions that have one clear right answer, such as multiple-choice questions), students and teachers can know immediately what they do and do not know.

If we want to know how students are thinking, then we have to give them an opportunity to explain what is behind what they are doing. Academic prompts can be verbal, written, or digitally recorded graphic explanations of a concept. Basically, anything that requires a student to expose their reasoning can function as an academic prompt, although these usually take the form of short-answer or essay questions.

As teachers, we need access to valid, reliable tests and prompts. We often complain about standardized tests, so if we want alternatives, we must be able to build our own. Valid, reliable tests are especially important if your school or district is building unit assessments for consequential decision-making across classes and campuses. Good assessments are a necessary precondition for good feedback.

While I was teaching intermediate and middle-grade students, I spent years writing science assessment items for a major test publisher for five states. While much of the work was tedious and had to go through four levels of review, the publisher paid $25 to $50 per accepted question, so I wrote hundreds. The items were multiple choice as well as extended-response items. As a word of warning, we were not allowed to use K–12 textbooks as source materials for our questions because there were too many errors in them. This was particularly disturbing because the test publisher was a division of a major textbook publisher. Our source material had to come from college textbooks or scientific agencies such as the National Aeronautics and Space Administration (NASA) or National Oceanic and Atmospheric Administration (NOAA). Having accurate source material is vital for validity and reliability and even more important to ensure that students are learning what they are supposed to be learning.

Multiple Choice

Below are a few quick tips that helped me write better multiple-choice items for my own classes that I learned from my time writing standardized items. When I was writing, these rules were the law because they were the only way the testing company would pay me for the items I wrote. Some of these are necessary for questions going into massive question banks that can be used in any combination so while they are less relevant to classroom assessments, they might be helpful for consistency and clarity (also see Box 7.2). Multiple-choice items should do the following:

1) Be sure to measure a standard. The question needs to be directly related to the content you are trying to teach.

2) Be appropriately difficult for the target population.

3) Be grammatically correct and easy to read. Be sure to pay attention to font. Assessments are not the time for cute font or font that is too small.

4) Be questions, not statements with blanks. This was a rule that really mattered because the items went into test banks, but there is some benefit to being consistent on our own assessments as well.

5) Have one clear, correct answer with three plausible distractors (the other choices). Be sure to vary the letter that corresponds to the correct answer (e.g., do not make *A* the correct answer for 12 consecutive questions). Sometimes teachers will pick the same answer consecutively to see if students are confident enough of their answers to pick the same letter repeatedly. This makes the formatting of the test beyond student understanding a variable on the test that reduces reliability and validity.

6) The answer and distractors should be of similar length and parallel structure.

7) Avoid questions that use *not, all of the above,* or *none of the above.* Think about this from the perspective of struggling test takers: The cognitive demand for the entire test is to find one right answer, but then these kinds of questions require them to find the wrong answer or more than one correct answer. If you are preparing students for law school and the LSAT, this makes sense, but most of the time, we are using multiple-choice tests to determine whether students know surface-level content.

8) Be a balance of clarity and economy. A science test should not be a reading test by being unnecessarily wordy. The principles of universal design should always be considered to make the test as accessible as possible to students.

9) Avoid long distractors. The bulk of the reading should be in the question.

10) Use as many graphics as possible.

7.2 Just Teaching Strategy

Build Valid, Reliable Multiple-Choice Items

Take one of the assessments that you are currently using, whether it is from a publisher, your district, or your own. Look at the multiple-choice items. Do many of them pass this checklist? If so, great news—you are well on your way to a valid, reliable test and maybe a job writing for a test publisher! If not, there is always room for improvement.

Matching

The summative assessment in one of my graduate classes was a 50-item matching test. There is so much wrong with this as a summative assessment, but I want to focus on a few common pitfalls this example highlights. First, a matching test of this length becomes a logic puzzle. Overlapping terms and concepts create challenges. If students misinterpret the instructor's intent with one definition, they create a domino effect of potentially incorrect answers. Second, the cognitive demand for attempting to differentiate 50 items is high. Students are struggling with the test format as much as the content. Third and probably most important, a matching test is unlikely to assess anything deeper than surface-level knowledge, and this was an assessment of a graduate school class for educators who wanted to improve curriculum and instruction.

While matching items are not ideal for an entire test, they certainly can be a component of a summative assessment. I do not recommend lists of more than ten items and would even break up lists of ten into two lists for students who struggle with reading. We have to remember that matching items are a snapshot of surface-level learning (see Box 7.3).

7.3 Just Teaching Strategy

Build Valid, Reliable Matching Items

Look at Matching Test #1 and Matching Test #2. Most matching tests that I see are arranged like #1. Why? I really do not know, but that is the way I see most matching tests.

(Continued)

(Continued)

Matching Test #1

1) ___ feedback	a. should be given well before the beginning of a unit
2) ___ summative assessment	b. describes criteria for success and performance levels
3) ___ formative assessment	c. given to improve performance through deliberate practice
4) ___ diagnostic assessment	d. given at the end of a learning segment to evaluate what students know and can do
5) ___ rubric	e. given throughout a learning segment to inform teachers and students of learning progress

Now look at Matching Test #2. Why is it better?

Matching Test #2

1) ___ should be given well before the beginning of a unit	a. feedback
2) ___ describes criteria for success and performance levels	b. summative assessment
3) ___ given to improve performance through deliberate practice	c. formative assessment
4) ___ given at the end of a learning segment to evaluate what students know and can do	d. diagnostic assessment
5) ___ given throughout a learning segment to inform teachers and students of learning progress	e. rubric

We read from left to right. A student who struggles with reading is going to take far longer with Matching Test #1. Because a matching test is not meant to be a reading test, simply shifting the reading load to the left makes a significant difference for the amount of time this will take students. Here's why: Struggling readers will read the first word, "feedback." Then they will read down the list of all five options. Next, they will read "summative assessment" and read down all five options again because they probably are not savvy enough to eliminate the choice they already made for "feedback."

Matching Test #2 loads most of the reading on the left side. If struggling students follow the exact process they used for Matching Test #1, they will read "Should be given well before the beginning of the unit" and then read each of the five options that are one or two words. Without reducing the content rigor of the test at all, we have made the matching items more accessible to a wider range of students. This is a justice issue. Test items should be as accessible as possible to as many students as possible.

True/False

If you are like me, you are wary of true/false items. How many of us have been burned by a true/false item that the teacher thought was true, but we identified an exception that made us mark it false? For example, suppose I created the following statement:

"True or False: Formative assessment helps us plan effective units for each student."

This statement is true, but given the way I have used the term, you might have correctly assumed that this more accurately describes *diagnostic assessment*. In this case, your understanding of a term is actually working against you getting credit for this answer. This invalidates the item and is unjust because I do not know all that you know and have actually used that knowledge against you.

Use true/false items sparingly. If you use them, give the student the opportunity to correct a false statement to make it true on the test so that you can see if they are engaged in some other higher-order consideration than you assumed would be possible on a given item. Additionally, you could ask students to defend their position in a short-answer response, which would help you get to deeper levels of thinking. Avoid using extreme words such as *always* or *never* that beg for students to find exceptions to the rule. Finally, do not make the items a test of student logic unless that is the purpose of the test.

Academic Prompts

Based on my assessment training, there are several considerations that will improve the questions that we write for extended student responses. First, extended responses, whether written or verbal, are great for getting at higher-order thinking. If we can encourage students to make a claim and then provide evidence for that claim, we get a glimpse into higher-order thought processes. For example, in a science class, if I ask a student to develop an experiment to test a boat designed to carry the maximum amount of weight within parameters and then conduct that experiment, I am going to learn a lot about their thinking by having them write a one-paragraph conclusion about their approach and their evidence of success or failure. Ideally, this could be part of a conversation, but time is the enemy of one-on-one conversations with students, so sometimes the written response or a digitally recorded explanation is the more reasonable approach.

Second, for students to speak or write strong extended responses, they need clear criteria for success in the form of a rubric or other parameters. We will dig into rubrics at the end of the chapter.

Third, students need training in how to produce extended responses. They need to

1) include the question in the formation of the thesis statement;

2) offer pertinent, succinct support; and

3) have a concluding statement.

The first and third steps are relatively easy to address. The second step is challenging and requires repeated practice, exposure to exemplars, and public revision of student work. Even in my science classes, we would take student responses, make them anonymous, and look at them on screen to determine if the support was pertinent, succinct, and comprehensive.

Fourth, we should use extended responses across all disciplines, including math. Particularly in a time when cheating seems to be pervasive, asking students to explain their work in their own words is essential for identifying what students know and can do. Having students record their work on apps such as Screencastify, Go Formative, or Loom allows teachers to see and hear these explanations asynchronously.

Performance Tasks

What we really want to move toward as just teachers are performance tasks. Performance tasks require students to explore the subject to the extent they are able. They are to use their basic knowledge and developing skills to be mathematicians, scientists, historians, or writers. For example, after conducting several lab experiments to build baseline knowledge, students would design and conduct their own scientific inquiry.

Performance tasks simplify our work because it is no longer about us. Our students become apprentices engaged in authentic, meaningful work that replicates what people in our disciplines do. We want to promote "productive failure" by allowing students to work on challenging problems because they drive deeper learning (Kapur, 2008). Good performance tasks are realistically contextualized, require judgment and innovation, and ask the student to "do" the subject with clearly identified criteria for success. Regardless of level, to the extent possible, we ask students to think like mathematicians, historians, scientists, engineers, authors, and editors. The work must be meaningful because performance tasks will take significant class time and require deep investment on the part of students. Two enormous benefits of performance tasks are that they allow multiple opportunities for feedback and they are a lot more interesting to assess than most tests and essays because we are truly seeing students' thinking and skills. In the eight-step feedback process in Chapter 6, teachers give feedback twice and students give feedback in the co-creation of the goals, to each other in peer review, to the teacher in the first final draft and the revisions, and finally through reflection. Feedback permeates the process.

> Two enormous benefits of performance tasks are that they allow multiple opportunities for feedback and they are a lot more interesting to assess than most tests and essays because we are truly seeing students' thinking and skills.

Consider this example from teacher preparation that many of you would be familiar with. I spent ten years preparing pre-service teachers. In almost every state in the country, there is some requirement for those pre-service candidates to take multiple-choice tests of basic and professional knowledge. However, these are not adequate for determining if they are ready to teach actual children. Therefore, we structured methods of teaching classes to give them the opportunity to develop learning experiences that they would test in simulations on their peers. They received significant feedback from professors and peers. Once we felt that they were ready to facilitate these learning experiences with real children, they had that opportunity under the supervision of an experienced classroom teacher in a practicum. They received feedback from students, supervising faculty, and the classroom teacher. This would build to student teaching, where they would be responsible for planning weeks of instruction under the supervision of the classroom teacher with significant feedback.

The performance tasks associated with preparing to teach are only as good as the opportunities and feedback we receive *and* apply. The same is true for each of our students in our disciplines. For our students to reach their goals, they must know the criteria for success (Hattie, 2012) and develop the skills, knowledge, and habits of mind that represent expertise in a given area—the true nature of an apprenticeship (see Box 7.4).

7.4 Just Teaching Strategy

Analyze Your Assessments

At the end of each unit, it is always good to spend five to ten minutes making notes about what could be better the next time. The best way to do that is to look at your assessments. If you have not done this at the end of the unit in a previous year, analyze assessments that you plan to give at the beginning of a unit to ensure alignment with standards and equity for each student. Regardless of the assessment type, ask yourself these three questions:

1. What would I change about the assessment?

2. What would I change about the unit?

3. How could each student demonstrate even deeper learning next year?

If you can answer these three questions, your next unit will be on the road to improvement.

Rubrics

One of the easiest ways to facilitate eight-step feedback is through clear rubrics. Rubrics support just teaching because they reduce bias and bring clarity (Quinn, 2020). Immediately after generating a new assessment idea, I write the rubric. This is important for at least two reasons. Writing the rubric requires me to (1) clearly articulate the criteria for success and (2) describe what varying degrees of success might look like. Writing the rubric with my students has also been a useful exercise for giving them ownership and ensuring they are clear on the criteria for success. While I much prefer the creative design of assessments and learning experiences, rubrics force me to discipline my thinking and provide clear parameters for student work.

Rubrics are an example of an effortless action that can lead to effortless results (McKeown, 2021). Once we have made a good rubric, we can simply modify it in subsequent years. More importantly, students are going to produce better work because they will be clearer about what good work requires. Here are a few basic guidelines for any type of rubric you write, adopt, or modify.

Be Sure It Is a Rubric and Not a Checklist

A rubric must describe levels that differentiate how students are performing based on clear criteria. A list of things an assignment should include with a point value next to it is a checklist, not a rubric. For example, a checklist for an essay might include a thesis statement (20 points), three body paragraphs (20 points each), and a conclusion (20 points). Checklists can be useful to ensure that critical elements are present, but they do not inform students about what success is.

Be Clear

Once students have read the rubric, they should know what success will look like. When I go over a rubric with students, we only address the column that tells them what they need to do to earn full credit.

Be Positive

When defining criteria and performance levels, describe what you want students to produce, not what is missing. For example, if students can earn a *4* for "providing four pieces of pertinent textual evidence that enhance their argument," then a *3* should be for "providing three to four pieces of pertinent textual evidence that somewhat enhance their argument." This should be continued for the *2* and the *1*. We should describe performance levels based on what we see instead of what we do not see. We should not describe the *4* and then identify the *3* as "missing pertinent textual evidence and/or does not connect evidence to argument." By writing what we want to see, students better understand what they need to do to improve.

Use a Three- or Four-Point Scale

Generally, I prefer to create four different performance levels because that allows me to differentiate student performance a bit more effectively than three levels. However, sometimes I have a really difficult time coming up with four distinct levels, so I settle for three. The key is to communicate to students how they are performing against the standard.

Do Not Give Credit When No Evidence Is Present

This is an important point for me. Zeroes are only problematic on the 100-point scale. On a three- or four-point scale, they have appropriate weight. If I am evaluating criteria, I want to be sure that I am only giving students credit if they have produced what they have been asked to do. They should not receive credit, even a *1*, if they have not provided any supporting evidence. I always leave a space for a *0* with a description of "no evidence."

Do Not Judge Effort or Creativity as Separate Criteria

Many rubrics include effort or creativity as discrete criteria. This is a problem on several levels. First, the criteria on the rubric should be measuring standards that are essential skills and knowledge. Second, effort and creativity should be the drivers of those skills and knowledge. For example, "providing pertinent textual evidence" to support a claim requires effort. "Communicating in an engaging manner" might require creativity. By evaluating those criteria, we are also implicitly assessing effort and creativity.

When we make effort and creativity discreet categories, we create an opportunity to perpetuate injustice. Here is what I mean. If we are assessing a shoebox diorama of a student's favorite scene from a book and we assess effort and creativity as their own categories, what are we actually assessing? First, this is a weak assessment of reading comprehension. Second, when students need resources to complete projects, those resources should be provided or the project should be completed at school. Otherwise, inequities are exacerbated. Third, creativity might look like coloring in the entire box, having figures or crafts from Hobby Lobby, using LEGO bricks to build structures, or having clay for different shapes. We might judge effort similarly. If that is the case, we are giving students points based on the availability of resources, how much a parent was willing to help, or how much someone was willing to spend to get this work done. Students without those resources are judged as not being creative or putting forth effort. This is injustice perpetrated by a poorly designed project and rubric.

> When we make effort and creativity discreet categories, we create an opportunity to perpetuate injustice.

In keeping with the spirit of making our work easier and not harder, there are three different ways to build a rubric. They require different amounts of work at different points in the assessment process.

For a single-point rubric, we write the criteria for success in the center column. I generally try to focus on four to five criteria. Once that is completed, we are finished. The challenge is that when we must assess student work, we have to write up evidence that exceeds or does not yet reach the standard if that is the case for different students; however, this will provide personalized feedback to each student, which could be a positive. We also must determine how we will score the student's work if we need to report a grade, as there are not performance levels included.

To help illustrate what this looks like, see Figure 7.4 as an example that I might use to evaluate this book chapter if it were an assignment. You can feel free to score my work, as these criteria represent what a successful chapter would look like for me. I know there is always room for improvement.

FIGURE 7.4   Single-Point Rubric

TOOL #7 | **RUBRIC WIZARD**

SINGLE-POINT RUBRIC

Areas that need work	Criteria for Success Standards for this performance task	Evidence of Exceptional Performance
	The chapter has a clear thesis that is pertinent to assessment and feedback for educators.	
	The structure of the chapter supports the reader in understanding the flow and organization of ideas with subheadings, boxes, and clear direction for the reader.	
	The author provides ample research support for the thesis with accessible application to educational settings.	
	The examples, questions, and exercises allow readers to engage and apply ideas to their contexts.	

During planning: *least work*   While assessing: *most work*

The holistic rubric is the middle ground of our three rubrics. This rubric requires some work on the front end as we have to decide what high-quality products would look like. We describe what success on the whole product would be and describe it in prose form. Then we describe what the next levels should be. When students submit their assessments, we can just circle the description that best fits their work, but this can be challenging as we might find ourselves underlining some aspects of the description in several different categories and trying to score the assignment a 3.75. This can be problematic for letting a student know how to improve, which will require some additional explanation from us that will take more time.

Figure 7.5 is an example of how I would create a holistic rubric for this chapter.

FIGURE 7.5   Holistic Rubric

TOOL #7 | **RUBRIC WIZARD**

HOLISTIC RUBRIC

Score	Description
4	The chapter has a clear thesis that is pertinent to assessment and feedback for educators. The structure of the chapter supports the reader in understanding the flow and organization of ideas with subheadings, boxes, and clear direction for the reader. The author provides ample research support for the thesis with accessible application to educational settings. The examples, questions, and exercises allow readers to engage and apply ideas to their contexts.
3	The chapter has a thesis that is pertinent to assessment or feedback for educators. The structure of the chapter provides some support for the reader in understanding the flow of ideas with subheadings, boxes, or clear direction for the reader. The author provides some research support for the thesis with some application to educational settings. The examples, questions, and exercises allow readers to engage and ideas in their contexts.
2	The chapter has a thesis that is pertinent to assessment or feedback for educators. The structure of the chapter provides minimal support for the reader with subheadings, boxes, or clear direction for the reader. There are examples, questions, or exercises for readers.
1	The chapter has a thesis. There is minimal structure to the chapter. There are disjointed examples, questions, or exercises for readers.
0	No evidence of writing.

The analytic rubric is the one that we are probably most familiar with because when it is done, it is the easiest to use and gives students the most actionable feedback. The drawback is that it takes the most work to build and typically requires some tinkering after its initial use. The reason the analytic rubric takes the most work is that you describe the performance levels for each criterion. This specificity provides the student with specific feedback, but we have to develop each criterion with specificity at four different performance levels. Again, we need to communicate clearly where students are performing against a standard, and four levels provide more of that specificity.

Analytic rubrics typically take me three times as long to write as the other two; however, I more than make up that time when I am actually evaluating student work because I can mark the performance level for each criterion and, without any additional feedback, students know what they need to do next. One additional support for this investment in what becomes more effortless feedback is that the analytic rubric is far easier for students to use for peer feedback. They can look for specific things under each criterion and focus their comments there rather than thinking about the entire project (holistic rubric) or having to provide feedback on what is approaching or exceeding a standard (single-point rubric).

Figure 7.6 provides an example of an analytic rubric to assess this chapter.

Why This All Matters

Assessment can seem like a very abstract thing—as a hoop to jump through to satisfy parents and administration. However, the performance tasks and feedback I gave pre-service teachers will have long-term ramifications for my family for years to come. As a professor preparing new teachers, I was well aware of parents' concerns about getting a new teacher for their child, even if they thought our program was a good one. I frequently told them, "We only graduate teachers whom I would want teaching my own child." In reality, this was the case for me. From third through fifth grade, my youngest daughter had beginning teachers as her classroom teachers. They were all teachers whom I had taught in at least three classes and I had supervised two of them through student teaching. I can honestly say that my daughter and our family are better for those three teachers who made mistakes but grew alongside their students and passionately poured themselves into students—including my daughter.

Assessment matters. We are preparing the leaders, teachers, thinkers, and doers that build our communities and protect democracies. Our feedback informs their habits, which lead to our collective goals that are far more important than grades.

FIGURE 7.6   Analytic Rubric

TOOL #7 | **RUBRIC WIZARD**

ANALYTIC RUBRIC

Criteria	0	1	2	3	4
Thesis	No evidence	The chapter minimally related to assessment or feedback.	The chapter has a limited thesis that is somewhat pertinent to assessment or feedback.	The chapter has a thesis that is pertinent to assessment or feedback for educators.	The chapter has a clear thesis that is pertinent to assessment and feedback for educators.
Structure	No evidence	The structure of the chapter is limited or hinders the reader's understanding of the ideas in the chapter.	The structure of the chapter minimally supports the reader in understanding ideas with subheadings, boxes, or direction for the reader.	The structure of the chapter somewhat supports the reader in understanding the organization of ideas with subheadings, boxes, or direction for the reader.	The structure of the chapter supports the reader in understanding the flow and organization of ideas with subheadings, boxes, and clear direction for the reader.
Evidence-based	No evidence	The author provides very limited research. support for the thesis.	The author provides minimal research support for the thesis with limited application to educational settings.	The author provides some research support for the thesis with application to educational settings.	The author provides ample research support for the thesis with accessible application to educational settings.
Application	No evidence	The examples, questions, or exercises minimally engage the reader.	The examples, questions, or exercises somewhat engage the reader.	The examples, questions, and exercises allow readers to engage ideas.	The examples, questions, and exercises allow readers to engage and apply ideas to their contexts.

During planning: *most work*   While assessing: *least work*

Just Teaching Tool #7
Rubric Wizard

If you worked on the authentic assessment (Just Teaching Tool #6) with a colleague, then continue that work.

1) Building on the authentic assessment you began to design at the end of Chapter 6, pick one of the three rubric options and write a rubric.

2) Be sure to positively describe what you want to see.

3) Identify at least three clear performance levels if you are writing a holistic or analytic rubric.

4) Check your criteria to be sure they measure what you intend and do not unnecessarily overlap.

5) Score your own authentic assessment.

6) Revise the rubric based on any holes you found in your own authentic assessment.

7) Share with students and get their feedback. Are the criteria clear? If applicable, are the performance levels clear?

8) Revise based on student feedback.

9) Assess! The first time I use a rubric to assess an entire class's assignments, I find holes. Be sure to revise.

(Continued)

(Continued)

TOOL #7 | **RUBRIC WIZARD**

SINGLE-POINT RUBRIC

Areas That Need Work	Criteria for Success Standards for this performance task	Evidence of Exceptional Performance

During planning: *least work*   While assessing: *most work*

TOOL #7 | **RUBRIC WIZARD**

HOLISTIC RUBRIC

Score	Description
4	
3	
2	
1	
0	

During planning: *least work*   While assessing: *most work*

SCAN THE QR CODE
FOR A FILLABLE PDF

(Continued)

(Continued)

TOOL #7 | **RUBRIC WIZARD**

ANALYTIC RUBRIC

Criteria	0	1	2	3	4

During planning: *least work*   While assessing: *most work*

Part IV

Thriving

In this final chapter, we will bring together all the tools and ideas you have generated around feedback, engagement, and well-being to help you grow the giants in your classroom in a sustainable, life-giving way. This is how we will build schools in which each student thrives.

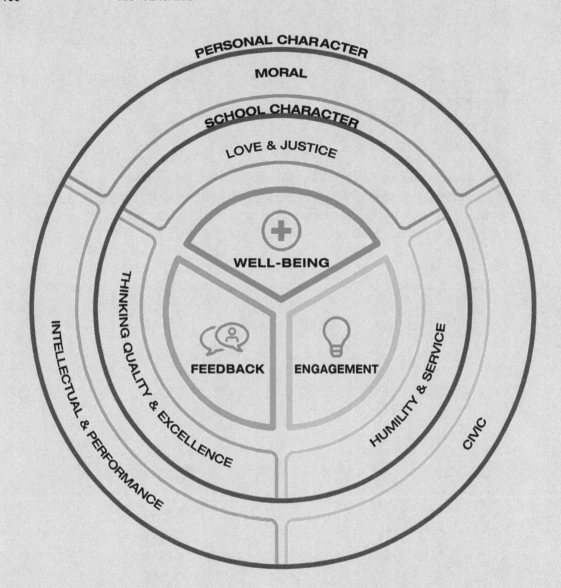

Growing Giants

8

And now these three remain: faith, hope, and love.
But the greatest of these is love.

I Corinthians 13:13

Just Teaching

Chapter 8. "Decomplexified"

- As educators, we are the critical element in schools.

- FEW (feedback, engagement, well-being) is a mutually reinforcing expression of love.

- Adaptive leadership with others changes mindsets that lead to improvement.

- While we are not superheroes, we need to wield our "deathless power" like Avengers and not like Batman.

- Growing giants requires confident humility and others.

- Catalysts accelerate the good work of others without being used up.

- Time is precious. Take time to savor the poignant moments.

Love

I have grounded this book in the essence of what education is: feedback, engagement, and well-being (FEW) for each student. Our desire to serve students in these three ways is rooted in a deep desire to see them thrive. That desire is rooted in faith, hope, and most importantly, love. What is most assuring about this is that this is not a new idea but is rooted in timeless truth. As you see in the figure at the beginning of Part IV, the way we address our FEW ideas ripples out into schools that are loving, just, humble, and excellent and that develop people of high moral, civic, performance, and intellectual virtue. In other words, we grow the giants we explored in Chapter 1.

So where are the roots of this desire for growing giants?

I was a senior in high school in a town that announced itself as the "Gateway to the Coalfields" on its chain-link welcome sign. Over the loud complaints of me and my brothers, my family had moved to West Virginia during my junior year of high school. We had a grocery store that sponsored bear wrestling in the parking lot, sewage that we dumped in the Little Coal River, coal mines, black lung clinics, and limited opportunities. We had Hatfields at our school who were descendants of the legendary Hatfield–McCoy feud. My best friend's father shot and killed his neighbors in a family feud that had lasted for years up their holler (an Appalachian term for a narrow valley). However, there were a couple of teachers at the high school who wanted more for us. They created places to take risks, engaged our minds in books and ideas, and pushed us to write more and go deeper with our work. I could not identify it at the time, but they were just teachers in the best sense of the term. Due to their efforts, I began to feel a tug toward teaching.

Because we were in a high-poverty area of Appalachia, I received a federal teaching scholarship with the caveat that I had to teach two years for every year I took the scholarship. I am now 20 years past my scholarship's contractual commitment to teaching. I am part of the profession that makes all others possible. We make professions accessible to students by knowing each student and shaping solutions that enhance their well-being, their engagement, and our feedback.

We are the decisive element. This is not a narcissistic, self-indulgent view of teaching. Neither is it overwhelming. Haim Ginott (1972, p. 15) wrote:

I have come to a frightening conclusion.

I am the decisive element in the classroom.

It is my personal approach that creates the climate.

It is my daily mood that makes the weather.

As a teacher I possess tremendous power to make a child's life miserable or joyous.

I can be a tool of torture or an instrument of inspiration.

I can humiliate or humor, hurt or heal.

In all situations, it is my response that decides whether a crisis will be escalated or de-escalated, and a student humanized or de-humanized.

I have taught elementary through graduate school students, and when I strip away what does not matter, I am left with feedback, engagement, and well-being. Teaching is human, essential, and can be life-giving. Teaching is an act of faith, hope, and love—and the greatest of these is love. We humanize teaching and leading when we answer the calling to love those around us. Policies, bureaucracies, requirements, frustrations, complaints, and everything that saps our joy falls away when we love others well.

Instead of draining us, that love fills us and overflows to others.

We create the climate and make the weather in our classrooms, schools, and districts.

We create the climate and make the weather in our classrooms, schools, and districts.

We can inspire, heal, and humanize.

We grow giants.

Love manifests itself in the mutually reinforcing elements of FEW. For example, in one study in which high school students gave motivational advice to younger students—advice such as how to stop procrastinating—the advice-givers earned higher report card grades in math and a self-selected target class (Eskreis-Winkler et al., 2019). The feedback about engagement and practices that support well-being enhanced outcomes for the students providing the feedback. While we have addressed the three elements of just teaching separately, at their best, they are intertwining parts of a learning ecosystem.

Remember the sequoia redwoods from Chapter 1? We are the interconnected roots of that massive, living, breathing community of interdependent life. As educators, we set the weather, deliver nutrients, and offer support; however, we do not do this alone.

What We Know Works: Adaptive Leadership Together

The best person I know for growing forests of thriving educators, Erik Ellefsen, shared these facts about the redwoods with me. He is a significant part of the forest that supports me and many educators. In many ways, his support expanded through his own suffering. In 2008, he was diagnosed with multiple myeloma and has been on chemotherapy for 13 years, having endured bone marrow transplants (yes, plural), more than 30 bone marrow biopsies, and remarkable suffering. The life expectancy for people with his diagnosis was two years. When he was first diagnosed, he had to step down from his role as principal, but he never lost his passion for education. That passion merely shifted. Not knowing how long or how much energy he had to lead, he began connecting others to do good work. He is always in the back of conferences, meetings, restaurants, and classrooms connecting good educators around meaningful work—intertwining redwood roots that tap into educators' "deathless power."

In *Like Captured Fireflies*, John Steinbeck (Shillinglaw & Benson, 2002) describes the power educators have. He is encouraging his 11-year-old son, who is tired of school. Steinbeck describes how students carry new ideas into classrooms "cupped and sheltered in our hands like captured fireflies" (p. 142). Each student, each idea, is precious and provides a precarious light source. He goes on to write about the teacher: "She left her signature upon us, the literature of the teacher who writes on children's minds." Note the intertwined nature of this interaction—one teacher, but many students and many minds—tapping the innate curiosity of each human being collectively. He concludes, "I've had many teachers who taught us soon forgotten things, but only a few like her who created in me a new thing, a new attitude, a new hunger. I suppose that to a large extent I am the unsigned manuscript of that teacher. What deathless power lies in the hands of such a person" (p. 143).

We do not create a "new thing, a new attitude, a new hunger" in others by believing that we have all the answers. Ronald Heifetz and colleagues (Heifetz, 1994; Heifetz et al., 2009; Heifetz & Linsky, 2017) research adaptive leadership. Adaptive leadership addresses challenges in which the problem and solution are unclear. Adaptive challenges require a change in mindset because the solution requires a more integrated approach. Improving learning outcomes for *each* student is an adaptive challenge for *each* student. Too often, policymakers have designed technical solutions to adaptive challenges, such as testing students more often to make students learn more. Technical solutions to adaptive problems do not address the root of the issue and create cynicism in people who are having the solutions enacted on them. This book is designed for adaptive improvement and is not meant to be a technical solution. We know that FEW must be personalized for whole human beings. Part of adaptive improvement is identifying technical solutions that can be combined and contextualized to meet individual student needs. Leadership, like teaching, becomes infinitely interesting when we see our work as adaptive and as something that we do with others (see Box 8.1).

8.1 Just Teaching Strategy

Use Adaptive Tools

At the Baylor Center for School Leadership (BCSL), we have developed five tools (beyond the ones in this book) that help you identify an adaptive challenge as a school team and then work toward adaptive improvement. These are not easy tools to use, as they require individuals and teams to peel back challenges to find their core. You can find the tools and their descriptions here. These tools are most effective as components of facilitated improvement communities, but here are few questions to get you started:

Tools for adaptive improvement

1. What is an adaptive challenge you face in the classroom?

2. What is an adaptive challenge that your school's leaders face?

3. How could focusing on FEW shift mindsets related to the adaptive challenge in your classroom or school?

What Works in Real Schools: Trust, Others, and Catalysts

This deathless power of educators is real. I see it every day with college students who are better because of teachers they had in elementary, middle, and high school. I see it in graduate students who are principals and superintendents because of the teams of teachers and administrators who poured into them. Throughout this book, we have seen the power that teams of educators can have on the lives of students. Here is one more example from an outstanding educator, Gabrielle Wallace, who sees adaptive improvement as something that requires trust, others, and culture change:

> As a first-year administrator in the Dallas area, I was asked to step in as an interim principal in the spring semester. Our [state] rating of an *F* resulted in a targeted team effort to create systems, school culture, and consistent practices. We believed that if we could change the adult culture at the school, hold students to high expectations socially, and build an academic culture within, everything else would fall into place.

> It wasn't just our ratings that changed. The confidence of our teachers and pride within our students elevated, too. For students, we implemented a restorative practice system that addressed all students every morning, including discipline issues and recurring suspensions. . . . We remembered everyone is human—they need support and encouragement in times of failure. Also, we celebrated together and cultivated the time to grow as a community.

> I wasn't always sure we were going to raise our rating beyond an *F*. However, key moments started to occur that helped me believe.

1) A 50-person humanities class with two teachers and an aide was fully implementing project-based learning (PBL). Every student was assigned to stations that addressed various learning needs. The teacher hosted workshops (small groups) to facilitate interventions. Students analyzed their data to write reflections and plans for growth. This was the same classroom where the teachers initially felt traditional teaching was the only option and resisted PBL. The classroom became a district-level example of strong instructional delivery that the superintendent endorsed.

2) A first-year teacher who was initially unsure of herself began to create more "experts" in her room. Students could now become content experts for peers to deliver feedback. To be an expert, the students had to refer to their notes to defend their explanations. While students were becoming experts, the teacher created a system to deliver three rounds of feedback to each student within a 90-minute block.

3) Structurally, the district provided a three-hour enrichment time for students once a week while teachers went into planning sessions with curriculum specialists and campus administration. Enrichment transferred from a secondary-level nap and snack time to one hour dedicated to academic computer-based interventions, restorative circles, and guest speakers or counselor lessons.

Our campus incorporated project-based learning and restorative practices to move our campus from a rating of 59 to 79 within a year. [This is the state rating system for each Texas school.] I have so many more moments of joy and wins to share from the campus. However, I wouldn't be honest if I did not mention all the injustices or inequities we constantly battled. This experience inspired me to intentionally seek out lived experience in other contexts and pursue a doctoral degree to understand systemic barriers. Both have confirmed that we were on the right track for serving communities and students.

Growing giants requires other giants to be the support we need. Gabrielle's practices changed as teachers and administrators began to trust others and this gave her insight into how to better address the essential FEW ideas that mattered. Notice her confident humility at the end. She describes the moments of joy while acknowledging that there is still far more work to do. Instead of being discouraged, she is using that as the fuel to pursue more learning and a deeper understanding of systems to better serve her community.

We need more Avengers and less Batman. If you are not as familiar with the Marvel Cinematic Universe or DC Comics, let me explain. Batman operates alone, in the dark, and seeks revenge as a solitary vigilante. The Avengers work with and depend on others to protect the world, universe, and now a multiverse. We need others. When Avengers begin to operate on their own, they invariably run into multiverse-ending problems.

What we need are everyday educators who work together to support each student. We don't really need superheroes at all, but we need to operate as teams on a mission to love each student well. Superheroes are fictionalized superhumans and what we need is very human.

I have spent the last eight years researching and supporting teachers and administrators who want to work together toward shared goals because this is my best hope for schools. At Baylor University, we run the BCSL built around these principles, have built and launched a master's program built on collective leadership, and are developing a PhD program to support effective leadership in schools. We are building improvement communities of school teams who are working on shared problems of practice through the BCSL and partners such as the Center for Teaching Quality (CTQ). The BCSL and CTQ do not provide schools with technical solutions to adaptive problems. I really do believe in this.

And yet I do not always practice it.

Just yesterday, a colleague asked me what he could do to help with some of my work. I responded, "I am just grateful that you have left me alone so I can get my work done." Note the personal possessives in the last sentence. As a recovering Enneagram 3 "Achiever," I do not like to give up control because I do not trust that others will do it well. My lack of trust is kryptonite to collective leadership. Lack of trust erodes the team and minimizes our individual and collective efficacy.

When we do not trust, we try to do everything . . . and we get ulcers. I grew my first ulcer in 2020 amid the pandemic in my first year at university as we were building a new center and other new programs during a hiring freeze while experiencing the most significant disruption to education in my lifetime. I led nearly 100 virtual professional learning sessions that year talking about the need for others, self-care, and well-being while I worked 80–90 hours a week as work moved home and blurred any boundaries I had.

Susan Cain (2022) describes what some of us do and what many high school and college students do as attempting to project an image of "effortless perfection" (p. 132). According to Cain, this term was coined at Duke University in 2003, and it is extremely prevalent at universities—particularly elite ones. The idea is that we should give the impression of "an easy grace" that allows you to be successful without really having to try that hard.

While the motivation that drove me to ulcers was more about control than effortless perfection, both erode trust. We are not authentic when we portray ourselves in ways that are not true. We do not build trust when we do not trust others to do good work. Trust is an essential component of school improvement (Bryk & Schneider, 2002). To use a scientific term, we need to be *catalysts*. As a former science teacher, I love catalysts. Catalysts, by definition, accelerate a reaction or work that is already occurring *without being used up*. The work is not about the catalyst! The catalyst accelerates the work in a *sustainable* way.

We don't need more control or effortless perfection. We need tools for tracking FEW (see Box 8.2), and we need authentic catalysts.

8.2 Just Teaching Strategy

Track FEW

If we want to know if we are catalyzing conditions that support FEW, we need data to tell us how we are doing. The best source of that information is our student feedback. Grant Morgan, a quantitative methodologist, and I have developed a student survey for tracking FEW. We have validated our own items in conjunction with publicly available items from validated measures (Balch, 2012; English et al., 2015; Ferguson & Danielson, 2014). You can see sample items and reach out using the QR code, if you are interested in tracking these data. Our team can give you an individual teacher identifier and get feedback to you based on your students' responses. We have developmentally appropriate versions for Grades K–2, 3–5, and 6–12. The survey takes less than five minutes and provides valuable data on how you are doing. Below are a few example probes from the survey:

Survey data tracking FEW

- Feedback: "My teacher knows when I understand and when I do not."
- Engagement: "In this class, we learn a lot almost every day."
- Well-being: "My class is a good place for learning."

We would love to build a national database of FEW data, and we benefit by helping you with meaningful data for your classes and schools.

Catalysts for Our Students

Educators who are catalysts attend to FEW. To accelerate the good work of others, a catalyst ensures that others are well, fully engaged, and receiving meaningful feedback. When these three conditions are met, people thrive. By laughing, engaging in true fun around meaningful content, and providing feedback in a timely, just way, we become catalysts for our students.

I hesitate to use a fictional example because there are so many amazing real-life examples, but the 2022 Academy Award Winner for Best Picture, *CODA*, captures the catalytic power of an educator in one scene that is less than three minutes long. The main character, Ruby, is a child of deaf adults (CODA) and is the only hearing member of her family. She joined the school choir but does not know if she actually sings well when she has this exchange with the choir director, Bernardo Villalobos. This is the slightly abbreviated version of their exchange:

Mr. Villalobos:	You can sing. You have no control, but your tone is lovely.
Ruby:	Thanks. It's my favorite thing.
Mr. Villalobos:	What are you doing next year?
Ruby:	I don't know. Working with my dad.
Mr. Villalobos:	No college?
Ruby:	I am not good at school. . . . I can't afford school.
Mr. Villalobos:	They have scholarships. How do you feel when you sing?
Ruby:	I don't know. It is hard to explain.
Mr. Villalobos:	Try. (Ruby signs a beautiful image of the freedom she feels when she sings.)
Mr. Villalobos:	You will need to sight-read and learn a classical piece [for an audition at an elite music school]. I will need you nights and weekends. I do not waste my time, so if I am offering, it is because I hear something.

He is telling Ruby who she is becoming. He is not telling her who he wants her to be. He is speaking truth directly into her life. In this one brief exchange, he is addressing her well-being, sparking engagement, and delivering feedback. Notice that he starts and ends with feedback: "You can sing" and "If I am offering, it is because I hear something."

He engages her by not letting her get away with saying, "I don't know. It is hard to explain." He responds with "Try," and she delivers a beautiful visual representation of what she feels.

He addresses her well-being when he helps her see that college might be possible by telling her that there are scholarships available. His confident belief in his ability to identify talent and that she has it also builds up a student who has never been able to get that feedback from home.

Like all great educators, Mr. Villalobos truly sees and hears Ruby. He sees and hears her in a way that no one has seen and heard her before. He is not missing the tree for the forest. He not only sees the potential giant in front of him with prodigious, untapped talent, but he also speaks truth into her life that will allow her to thrive and become the giant she was meant to be.

This is the best part of what we get to do as administrators and teachers. We breathe life into students when we tell them who they are becoming. We need other adults who do the same for us. We need to be those adults for others.

Catalysts for Educators

How do we breathe life, fan flames, grow giants—pick your metaphor—in other educators? The same way we do for our students: We love them well. To love them well, we must have faith in them and hope that they can improve, but we show them love by telling them who they are becoming and supporting them along the way. For many of us, we find it easier to do this with students than with other adults (see Box 8.3). Maybe an example will spark your thinking. Ann Byrd is a National Board-Certified teacher and the President of the CTQ. I have worked with her for over a decade and have seen the way she catalyzes the work of others through her personal interactions and CTQ. She continues to go back into the classroom and teach (Eckert & Byrd, 2012), she leads an organization alongside educators, and she has devoted CTQ's work to cultivating the collective leadership of teachers and administrators to support thriving schools. Ann is one of the best facilitators I know because she elicits educators' best thinking by not being the center of professional learning. She makes the educators' ideas the center. The through line for all her work is catalyzing the work of educators.

8.3 Just Teaching Strategy

Show Love

To see how well you are loving others, answer these five questions.

This month, what is something you have done to show love to

1. a student?

2. a teacher?

3. an administrator?

4. a parent of a student?

5. yourself?

(Continued)

> (Continued)
>
> If you are like me, I have many examples for #1 and my examples become increasingly difficult to identify from #2–#5. Work on that this week. Remember to start with yourself, because you cannot love others well if you do not have margin. This is not another task; loving yourself and others liberates you to teach and lead well.

We do not need superheroes who are going to burn out or star in fictional movies about teaching. We need catalysts. The difference is clear in Figure 8.1.

FIGURE 8.1   Superheroes vs. Catalysts

SUPERHEROES	CATALYSTS
Arrogant	Confidently humble
Work is about me	Work is about others
Individual	Team
Exhausting	Life-giving
Burned out	Joyful

Catalysts are confidently humble in their work with other colleagues because they know that the work they are doing is not about them. Their self-worth is not tied to a superhero status that means that they must be valued or at the center of the work. Catalysts focus on their teams and accelerate others' work because they are even more excited by others' ideas than their own. The work becomes life-giving when many hands make the work lighter and the solutions we look for roll down the easier path instead of uphill. Instead of burning out, catalysts are joyful partners in meaningful work that leads to connection between humans and purpose.

Just Teaching Tool #8
Life-giving Solutions for Each Student

If you have completed all seven tools from each chapter, you should be well on your way to solutions for each student. I hope they feel less exhausting to you because these solutions are essential to our work and become life-giving when we find joy in the journey we walk with students. This score is not a ranking but is meant to be a way to identify where you and I can continue to grow!

For this tool, you need one summary statement from several tools. This can be a word or phrase and no more than a sentence. Then rate each tool based on your role and unit of analysis (e.g., student, class, school, or district). You can also complete this online.

Thanks for being just teachers and administrators. We are so grateful for you!

(Continued)

(Continued)

TOOL #8 | "EFFORTLESS" SOLUTIONS

A SUMMARY OF YOUR COMPLETED 7 TOOLS

INCLUDE A SUMMARY STATEMENT FOR TOOLS 1-7 AND THEIR RESPECTIVE SCORE

TOOL 1 | FOUR LENSES

What is a next step you identified for one student? How well does that next step align with Tools #2-#7? (0=Not at all, 100=Perfectly aligned)

NEXT STEP _____   SCORE _____ /100

TOOL 2 | WELL-BEING THERMOMETER

What is the temperature of your class, school, or district?

SCORE _____ /98

TOOL 3 | NORM GENERATOR

What is one habit, norm, and ritual you will cultivate to improve the well-being of your class, school, or district? How much will the habit, norm, and ritual improve learning? (0=Not at all, 33=Total gamechanger) rate each and then total

HABIT _____   _____ /33

NORM _____   _____ /33

RITUAL _____   _____ /33

SCORE _____ /99

TOOL 4 | DIGITAL TOOL BELT

What is one digital tool you are excited to use for the individual student you identified?
Class? School? District? How effectively did the tool work for the student, class, school, or district?
(0=Not effective, 100=Greatest tool ever)

TOOL FOR STUDENT _____ SCORE _____ /100

TOOL FOR CLASS/SCHOOL/DISTRICT _____ SCORE _____ /100

TOOL 5 | SELF & PEER REFLECTOR

What was your total score for items #1-12? SCORE _____ /120

TOOL FOR CLASS/SCHOOL/DISTRICT _____ SCORE _____ /100

TOOL 6 | AUTHENTIC ASSESSMENT DESIGNER

On scale of 0-100, (0=I would rather get a colonoscopy,
100=Students are going to demonstrate skills and knowledge in amazing ways),
what is your excitement level about your assessment?

SCORE _____ /100

TOOL 7 | RUBRIC WIZARD

On scale of 0-100 (0=I have no idea what students know and can do,
100=I have fully captured all relevant content and can differentiate performance levels
validly and reliably), how effective will your rubric be for providing student feedback?

SCORE _____ /100

**TOTAL SCORE FROM
TOOLS 1-7 ABOVE** /817

650-717: Celebrate what you are doing with students!

600-649: Students will be better because of what you are doing together!

500-599: Which area needs more energy from your students to make
your teaching/leadership feel more life-giving?

0-499: Where did the tools fail you?
Help us make them better at (insert QR Code and website).

SCAN THE QR CODE
FOR A FILLABLE PDF

Epilogue

Focus on What's Essential

*The average human lifespan is absurdly, terrifyingly,
insultingly short. . . . Assuming you live to be 80,
you'll have had about four thousand weeks.*

Oliver Burkeman (2021, p. 3)

In his book, *Four Thousand Weeks,* Oliver Burkeman recommends that we spend more time enjoying, savoring, and making the time we have meaningful and less time trying to manage it. One of the best ways to do this is to remind ourselves of how fleeting our time is.

So, I read the obituaries in the newspaper headlines that come to my phone every morning. Most of the time, I do not know the "famous" people the editors choose to remember and memorialize. I do not read them because I hope that one day the editors will choose to remember me, because that would mean I would be dead and I am certain I will not care at that point. Reading the obituaries each morning breathes meaning, purpose, and appreciation into my life. The obituaries remind me that life is finite and that each moment is a blessing that I can use in a meaningful way or that I can squander and never get back.

In her book, *Bittersweet: How Sorrow and Pain Make Us Whole* (2022), Susan Cain highlights the work of Dr. Laura Carstensen, a Stanford professor who studies life span and longevity. Understanding that life is finite and that precious moments end creates a sense of poignancy—feeling happy and sad at the same time. Poignancy causes us to savor and focus on what matters most. Poignancy is the feeling I get at the end of a good book. Poignancy is the end of a school year when our time together as a class ends. Reading obituaries each morning is my way of reminding myself that life is precious. I believe in the deathless power that Steinbeck describes (Shillinglaw & Benson, 2002) and that the work we do, the relationships we build, and the love we give echo in eternity. This does not weigh me down. This is freeing. Our work becomes a life-giving offering when we remove pretense and policy and we can focus on each student's well-being, engagement, and feedback.

Do not finish reading this book and believe that you have another to-do list to complete. If you are feeling overwhelmed, read the one-page Appendix in this book. This is the whole book decomplexified into one page. This is appropriate because I learned at the U.S. Department of Education that politicians wanted everything as a "one-pager."

The ideas in this book will make your life easier by focusing on what is most essential and enjoying the work.

The work is now yours. Take the tools at the end of each chapter and begin to shape solutions for each student in your care. Hopefully, you know by now that this work is better when you walk this journey with others, so grab some colleagues if you have not already. Be sure to include teachers and administrators because we learn and teach best together. Thanks for walking with me this far as we grow giants with faith, hope, and love.

After all, we are *just* teachers.

Appendix

Just Teaching "Decomplexified"
(The Whole Book as a "One Pager"!)

Chapter 1: Each Before All

- To serve each student, educators must attend to a FEW (feedback, engagement, and well-being) ideas.

- Just teaching does not have to be exhausting.

- Like sequoia redwoods, we grow best when we grow in networks of rooted relationships.

Chapter 2: Maslow Before Bloom

- Purpose-driven flourishing is the goal of education and is for the common good.

- Attending to well-being is not additional work; instead, it is the way we do our work.

- We need less cortisol and more serotonin, dopamine, and oxytocin.

Chapter 3: Humans Before Outcomes

- Identify what you and your school are known for. This is more than a mission statement.

- Identify what you would like to be known for.

- Establish personal, classroom, and school norms and habits that lead to thriving human beings.

Chapter 4: Cs Before As

- Engagement is about finding joy.

- Engagement requires four Cs: content, consolidation, collaboration, and creation.

- Before grading, ensure students are engaged.

Chapter 5: Inviting Before Demanding

- Fun and flow can be a part of deliberate practice.

- Fill the space in our classrooms to make more space for our students.

- Celebrate quirkiness and growth but not days off.

Chapter 6: Habits Before Goals

- Micro-changes in daily habits that we regularly assess transform lives.

- Eight-step feedback focuses us on students and their work.

- Elevate habits to rituals by regularly giving public feedback on culture-building contributions.

Chapter 7: Feedback Before Grades

- Assessment is more than judgment and evaluation.

- We need to create and use valid, reliable, and timely assessments.

- Assessment is a continuum and facilitates feedback.

Chapter 8: Growing Giants

- FEW is a mutually reinforcing expression of love.

- As educators, we are the critical element in schools and we build thriving communities.

- Adaptive leadership requires others, changed mindsets, and confident humility.

- Time is precious. Take time to savor the poignant moments.

References

Armenta, C. N., Fritz, M. M., & Lyubomirsky, S. (2017). Functions of positive emotions: Gratitude as a motivator of self-improvement and positive change. *Emotion Review*, 9(3), 183–190. https://doi.org/10.1177/1754073916669596

Balch, R. T. (2012). *The validation of a student survey on teacher practice*. Vanderbilt University Institutional Repository.

Baysen, E., Baysen, F., & Çakmak, N. (2020). Phenomenographic approach to teachers' wait-time use: Reasons and consequences. In D. Flaut, Š. Hošková-Mayerová, C. Ispas, F. Maturo, & C. Flaut (Eds.), *Decision making in social sciences: Between traditions and innovations* (pp. 203–221). Springer International Publishing. https://doi.org/10.1007/978-3-030-30659-5_12

Bernstein, J., Shore, J., & Lazar, D. (2019). Improving the rhythm of your collaboration. *MIT Sloan Management Review*. https://sloanreview.mit.edu/article/improving-the-rhythm-of-your-collaboration/

Bloom, B. S., Engehart, M. D., Furst, E. J., Hill, V. H., & Krathwohl, D. R. (1956). *Taxonomy of educational objectives*. Longmans Green.

Boser, U., Wilhelm, M., & Hanna, R. (2014). *The power of the Pygmalion effect: Teachers' expectations strongly predict college completion* (No. ED564606). Center for American Progress. https://eric.ed.gov/?id=ED564606

Bransford, J., Brown, A. L., Cocking, R. R., & Council, N. R. (2000). *How people learn: Brain, mind, experience, and school* (Expanded edition). National Academy Press.

Brooks, A. (2021). The real reason kids don't like school. *The Atlantic*. https://www.theatlantic.com/family/archive/2021/08/how-help-kids-like-school-better-loneliness/619881/

Brooks, D. (2019). *The second mountain: The quest for a moral life*. Random House.

Brown, B. (2012). *Daring greatly: How the courage to be vulnerable transforms the way we live, love, parent, and lead*. Avery.

Brown, P. C., Roediger, H. L., & McDaniel, M. A. (2014). *Make it stick: The science of successful learning*. Belknap Press.

Bryk, A. S., Gomez, L. M., Grunow, A., & LeMahieu, P. G. (2015). *Learning to improve: How America's schools can get better at getting better*. Harvard Education Press.

Bryk, A., & Schneider, B. (2002). *Trust in schools: A core resource for improvement*. Russell Sage Foundation.

Buechner, F. (1973). *Wishful thinking: A theological ABC*. Harper Collins.

Burkeman, O. (2021). *Four thousand weeks: Time management for mortals*. Farrar, Straus and Giroux.

Cain, S. (2012). *Quiet: The power of introverts in a world that can't stop talking*. Crown Publishers.

Cain, S. (2022). *Bittersweet: How sorrow and longing make us whole*. Crown.

Clear, J. (2018). *Atomic habits: An easy and proven way to build good habits and break bad ones*. Avery.

Cook, C. R., Coco, S., Zhang, Y., Fiat, A. E., Duong, M. T., Renshaw, T. L., Long, A. C., & Frank, S. (2018). Cultivating positive teacher–student relationships: Preliminary evaluation of the Establish–Maintain–Restore (EMR) method. *School Psychology Review*, *47*(3), 226–243. https://doi.org/10.17105/SPR-2017-0025.V47-3

Cook, C. R., Fiat, A., Larson, M., Daikos, C., Slemrod, T., Holland, E. A., Thayer, A. J., & Renshaw, T. (2018). Positive greetings at the door: Evaluation of a low-cost, high-yield proactive classroom management strategy. *Journal of Positive Behavior Interventions*, *20*(3), 149–159. https://doi.org/10.1177/1098300717753831

Cooper, P. J., & Simonds, C. J. (2007). *Communication for the classroom teacher* (Version 8, 8th ed.). [Computer software]. Pearson.

Czikszentmihalyi, M. (1990). *Flow: The psychology of optimal experience*. HarperPerennial.

Deci, E., & Flaste, R. (1995). *Why we do what we do: Understanding self-motivation*. Penguin Group, Inc.

Deming, W. E. (1993). Deming Four Day Seminar. Phoenix, AZ. https://blog.deming.org/2015/02/a-bad-system-will-beat-a-good-person-every-time/

Dorn, E., Hancock, B., Sarakatsannis, J., & Viruleg, E. (2021). *COVID-19 and education: An emerging K-shaped recovery*. McKinsey & Company. https://www.mckinsey.com/industries/education/our-insights/covid-19-and-education-an-emerging-k-shaped-recovery

Dubner, S. J. (Host). (2020, December 16). How do you cure a compassion crisis? (No. 444). [Audio podcast episode]. In *Freakonomics Radio*. https://freakonomics.com/podcast/how-do-you-cure-a-compassion-crisis-ep-444/

Duckworth, A. (2016). *Grit: The power of passion and perseverance*. Scribner.

Dweck, C. S. (2006). *Mindset: The new psychology of success*. Ballantine Books.

Eckert, J. (2016a). Bring joy back into the classroom. *Education Week*.

Eckert, J. (2016b). *The novice advantage: Fearless practice for every teacher*. Corwin Press.

Eckert, J. (2018). *Leading together: Teachers and administrators improving student outcomes*. Corwin Press.

Eckert, J., & Byrd, P. A. (2012). A different kind of education gap. *Phi Delta Kappan*, *94*(4), 49–52.

Eckert, J. M., & Dabrowski, J. (2010). Should value-added measures be used for performance pay? *Phi Delta Kappan*, *91*(8), 88–92.

Emdin, C. (2016). *For white folks who teach in the hood and the rest of y'all too: Reality pedagogy and urban education*. Beacon Press.

English, D., Burniske, J., Meibaum, D., & Lachlan-Hache, L. (2015). *Uncommon measures: Student surveys and their use in measuring teaching effectiveness*. American Institutes for Research. https://www.air.org/sites/default/files/Uncommon-Measures-Student-Surveys-Guidance-Nov-2015.pdf

Ericsson, K. A., Krampe, R. T., & Tesch-Romer, C. (1993). The role of deliberate practice in the acquisition of expert performance. *Psychological Review*, *100*(3), 363–406.

Eskreis-Winkler, L., Milkman, K. L., Gromet, D. M., & Duckworth, A. L. (2019). A large-scale field experiment shows giving advice improves academic outcomes for the advisor. *Proceedings of the National Academy of Sciences of the United States of America*, *116*(30), 14808–14810. https://doi.org/10.1073/pnas.1908779116

FAIR Health. (2021). *Impact of COVID-19 on pediatric mental health*. FAIR Health. https://s3.amazonaws.com/media2.fairhealth.org/whitepaper/asset/The%20Impact%20of%20COVID-19%20on%20Pediatric%20Mental%20Health%20-%20A%20Study%20of%20Private%20Healthcare%20Claims%20-%20A%20FAIR%20Health%20White%20Paper.pdf

Ferguson, R. F., & Danielson, C. (2014). How framework for teaching and tripod 7Cs evidence distinguish key components of effective teaching. In T. J. Kane, K. A. Kerr, & R. C. Pianta (Eds.), *Designing teacher evaluation systems: New guidance from the Measures of Effective Teaching Project* (pp. 98–143). Jossey-Bass.

Fullan, M., Quinn, J., & McEachen, J. (2018). *Deep learning: Engage the world, change the world.* Corwin.

Ginott, H. (1972). *Teacher and child: A book for parents and teachers.* Macmillan.

Gladwell, M. (2008). *Outliers: The story of success.* Bay Back Books.

Goldhaber, D., Kane, T., & McEachin, A. (2021). Analysis: Pandemic learning loss could cost U.S. students $2 trillion in lifetime earnings. What states and schools can do to avert this crisis. *The 74.* https://www.the74million.org/article/analysis-pandemic-learning-loss-could-cost-u-s-students-2-trillion-in-lifetime-earnings-what-states-schools-can-do-to-avert-this-crisis/

Grand View Research. (2021). *Team collaboration software market size, share and trends analysis report by software type, by application, by deployment, and segment forecasts, 2021-2028* (GVR-2-68038-633-2; p. 140). Grand View Research. https://www.grandviewresearch.com/industry-analysis/team-collaboration-software-market

Grant, A. (2016). *Originals: How non-conformists move the world.* Penguin.

Grant, A. (2018). *The Daily Show's secret to creativity* (Episode 2). https://www.ted.com/talks/worklife_with_adam_grant_the_daily_show_s_secret_to_creativity/transcript

Grant, A. (2021). *Think again: The power of knowing what you don't know.* Viking.

Hammond, Z. (2015). *Culturally responsive teaching and the brain.* Corwin.

Harding, S., Morris, R., Gunnell, D., Ford, T., Hollingworth, W., Tilling, K., Evans, R., Bell, S., Grey, J., Brockman, R., Campbell, R., Araya, R., Murphy, S., & Kidger, J. (2019). Is teachers' mental health and wellbeing associated with students' mental health and wellbeing? *Journal of Affective Disorders, 242,* 180–187. https://doi.org/10.1016/j.jad.2018.08.08010.1016/j.jad.2018.08.080

Harris, J. (2018, July 9–10). *Keynote.* Visible Learning Conference, Chicago, IL.

Hattie, J. (2009). *Visible learning: A synthesis of over 800 meta-analyses relating to achievement.* Routledge.

Hattie, J. (2012). *Visible learning for teachers: Maximizing impact on learning.* Routledge.

Hattie, J., & Yates, G. (2014). *Visible learning and the science of how we learn.* Routledge.

Heath, C., & Heath, D. (2017). *The power of moments.* Simon & Schuster.

Heifetz, R. (1994). *Leadership without easy answers.* Harvard University Press.

Heifetz, R. A., & Linsky, M. (2017). *Leadership on the line: Staying alive through the dangers of change.* Harvard Business Review Press.

Heifetz, R. A., Linsky, M., & Grashow, A. (2009). *The practice of adaptive leadership: Tools and tactics for changing your organization and the world.* Harvard Business Press.

Heller, R. (2017). On the science and teaching of emotional intelligence: An interview with Marc Brackett. *Phi Delta Kappan.* https://kappanonline.org/science-teaching-emotional-intelligence-interview-marc-brackett/?utm_source=PDK+International&utm_campaign=bf0aea04ff-Kappan_Newsletter_Lapsed_2_25_2020_COPY_01&utm_medium=email&utm_term=0_867590cd6a-bf0aea04ff-30152681&mc_cid=bf0aea04ff&mc_eid=7b4c3e3594

Herrmann, Z. (2018, September 5). A strategy for effective student collaboration. *Edutopia.* https://www.edutopia.org/article/strategy-effective-student-collaboration

Hess, F. (2018). Education reforms should obey Campbell's Law. *Education Next.* https://www.educationnext.org/education-reforms-obey-campbells-law/

Holt-Lunstad, J., Smith, T. B., Baker, M., Harris, T., & Stephenson, D. (2015). Loneliness and social isolation as risk factors for mortality: A meta-analytic review. *Perspectives on Psychological Science, 10*(2), 227–237. https://doi.org/10.1177/1745691614568352

Ivey-Stephenson, A. Z., Demissie, Z., Crosby, A. E., Stone, D. M., Gaylor, E., Wilkins, N., Lowry, R., & Brown, M. (2020). Suicidal ideation and behaviors among high school students—Youth risk behavior survey, United States, 2019. *MMWR Supplement, 69,* 47–55. http://doi.org/10.15585/mmwr.su6901a6external icon

Jackson, C. K., Porter, S., Easton, J. Q., & Kiguel, S. (2020). *Who benefits from attending effective schools? Examining heterogeneity in high school impacts* (No. 28194). National Bureau of Economic Research. https://doi.org/10.3386/w2819

Jackson, R. R. (2009). *Never work harder than your students: And other principles of great teaching.* Association for Supervision and Curriculum Development.

Johnson, M. (2020). *Flash feedback: Responding to student writing better and faster—Without burning out.* Corwin.

Johnson, Z. D., & LaBelle, S. (2017). An examination of teacher authenticity in the college classroom. *Communication Education*, *66*(4), 423–439. https://doi.org/10.1080/03634523.2017.1324167

Kapur, M. (2008). Productive failure. *Cognition and Instruction*, *26*(3), 379–425. JSTOR.

Karpicke, J. D. (2012). Retrieval-based learning: Active retrieval promotes meaningful learning. *Current Directions in Psychological Science*, *21*(3), 157–163.

Kirschner, P. A., Sweller, J., & Clark, R. (2006). Why minimal guidance during instruction does not work: An analysis of the failure of constructivist, discovery, problem-based, experimental, and inquiry-based teaching. *Educational Psychologist*, *41*, 75–86.

Kraft, M. A., Blazar, D., & Hogan, D. (2018). The effect of teacher coaching on instruction and achievement: A meta-analysis of the causal evidence. *Review of Educational Research*, *88*(4), 547–588. https://doi.org/10.3102/0034654318759268

Kumar, S., Martin, F., Budrani, K., & Ritzhaupt, A. (2019). Award-winning faculty online teaching practices: Elements of award-winning courses. *Online Learning Journal*, *23*(4), 160–180.

Kurtz, H. (2021, October 14). Higher student morale linked to in-person instruction, survey shows. *Education Week*. https://www.edweek.org/leadership/higher-student-morale-linked-to-in-person-instruction-survey-shows/2021/10

Kyndt, E., Raes, E., Lismont, B., Timmers, F., Cascallar, E., & Dochy, F. (2013). A meta-analysis of the effects of face-to-face cooperative learning. Do recent studies falsify or verify earlier findings? *Educational Research Review*, *10*, 133–149. https://doi.org/10.1016/j.edurev.2013.02.002

Lamothe, M., Boujut, E., Zenasni, F., & Sultan, S. (2014). To be or not to be empathic: The combined role of empathic concern and perspective taking in understanding burnout in general practice. *BMC Family Practice*, *15*(1), 15. https://doi.org/10.1186/1471-2296-15-15

Lemov, D. (2021). *Teach like a champion 3.0: 63 techniques that put students on the path to college.* Jossey-Bass.

Lewis, C. S. (2001). *The abolition of man.* Harper Collins.

Luks, A. (1998). Helper's high: Volunteering makes people feel good, physically and emotionally. *Psychology Today*, *22*(10), 39–42.

Mali, T. (2002). *What learning leaves.* Hanover Press.

Maslow, A. (1954). *Motivation and personality.* Harper and Row.

Mathewson, T. G. (2020, May 2). Is online school program backed by Facebook's Mark Zuckerberg the answer for coronavirus closures? *USA Today*. https://www.usatoday.com/story/news/education/2020/05/02/coronavirus-facebook-mark-zuckerberg-online-school-summit-learning/3046823001/

Matson, T., & Clark, J. (2020). *Improve student outcomes by building caring faculty relationships.* Gallup.

McCabe, D. L., Butterfield, K. D., & Trevino, L. K. (2012). *Cheating in college: Why students do it and what educators can do about it.* JHU Press.

McKeown, G. (2014). *Essentialism.* Currency.

McKeown, G. (2021). *Effortless.* Currency.

McTighe, J., & Silver, H. F. (2020). *Teaching for deeper learning: Tools to engage students in meaning making.* ASCD.

McTighe, J., & Willis, J. (2019). *Upgrade your teaching: Understanding by design meets neuroscience.* ASCD.

Meltzer, A., Quintero, D., & Valant, J. (2019). *Better serving the needs of America's homeless students.* The Brookings

Institution. https://www.brookings.edu/blog/brown-center-chalkboard/2019/10/24/better-serving-the-needs-of-americas-homeless-students/

Merriam-Webster. (2010). Sarcasm. *Merriam-Webster*. https://www.merriam-webster.com/word-of-the-day/sarcasm-2010-05-04

Minahan, J. (2019). Building positive relationships with students struggling with mental health. *Phi Delta Kappan, 100*(6), 56–59.

Moeller, J., Brackett, M. A., Ivcevic, Z., & White, A. E. (2020). High school students' feelings: Discoveries from a large national survey and an experience sampling study. *Learning and Instruction, 66,* 101301. https://doi.org/10.1016/j.learninstruc.2019.101301

National Academies of Sciences, Engineering & Medicine. (2018). *How people learn II: Learners, contexts, and cultures*. The National Academies Press. https://doi.org/10.17226/24783

Newton, D. (2020, August 7). Another problem with shifting education online: A rise in cheating. *Washington Post.* https://www.washingtonpost.com/local/education/another-problem-with-shifting-education-online-a-rise-in-cheating/2020/08/07/1284c9f6-d762-11ea-aff6-220dd3a14741_story.html

Nottingham, J., & Nottingham, J. (2017). *Challenging learning through feedback.* Corwin.

Palmer, P. (1998). *The courage to teach.* Jossey-Bass.

Pan, S. C., & Sana, F. (2021). Pretesting versus posttesting: Comparing the pedagogical benefits of errorful generation and retrieval practice. *Journal of Experimental Psychology: Applied, 27*(2), 237–257. https://doi.org/10.1037/xap0000345

Paul, A. M. (2021). *The extended mind: The power of thinking outside the brain.* Houghton Mifflin Harcourt.

Pawlo, E., Lorenzo, A., Eichert, B., & Ellis, M. J. (2019). All SEL should be trauma-informed. *Phi Delta Kappan, 101*(3), 37–41.

Phi Delta Kappan. (2019). *PDK poll of the public's attitudes toward the public schools.* https://pdkpoll.org/wp-content/uploads/2020/05/pdkpoll51-2019.pdf

Pierson, R. (2013, May 13). *Every kid needs a champion* [Video]. TED Conferences. https://www.ted.com/talks/rita_pierson_every_kid_needs_a_champion?language=en

Pondisco, R. (2021). Education's enduring love affair with "luxury beliefs." *Thomas B. Fordham Institute.* https://fordhaminstitute.org/national/commentary/educations-enduring-love-affair-luxury-beliefs

Price, C. (2021). *The power of fun: How to feel alive again.* The Dial Press.

Prothero, A. (2020, March 30). How to teach social-emotional learning when students aren't in school. *Education Week.* https://www.edweek.org/leadership/how-to-teach-social-emotional-learning-when-students-arent-in-school/2020/03?cmp=eml-eb-SEL-rccur-05142020&M=59612837&U=&UUID=c12 1423 ad13 b02a7cdee7c974f3a82fa

Quinn, D. M. (2020). Experimental evidence on teachers' racial bias in student evaluation: The role of grading scales. *Educational Evaluation and Policy Analysis, 42*(3), 375–392. https://doi.org/10.3102/0162373720932188

Riess, H., & Neporent, L. (2018). *The empathy effect: Seven neuroscience-based keys for transforming the way we live, love, work, and connect across differences.* Sounds True.

Rowe, M. B. (1969). Science, silence and sanctions. *Science and Children, 6*(6), 11–13.

Rowe, M. B. (1972). *Wait-time and rewards as instructional variables: Their influence on language, logic, and fate control.* National Association for Research in Science Teaching, Teachers College. https://www.semanticscholar.org/paper/Wait-Time-and-Rewards-as-Instructional-Variables%3A-Rowe/8f9e383153efd8edeb7b04a5cfa0595772ca2a58

Rowe, M. B. (1986). Wait time: Slowing down may be a way of speeding up! *Journal of Teacher Education, 37*(1), 43–50.

Seligman, M. E. P. (2011). *Flourish: A visionary new understanding of happiness and well-being.* Free Press.

Shillinglaw, S., & Benson, J. J. (Eds.). (2002). *America and Americans.* Viking.

Smith, R., & Lambert, M. (2008). Assuming the best. *Educational Leadership, 66*(1), 16–21.

Smylie, M. A., Murphy, J., & Louis, K. S. (2020). *Caring school leadership.* Corwin.

Sousa, D., & Tomlinson, C. A. (2011). *Differentiation and the brain: How neuroscience supports the learner-friendly classroom.* Solution Tree Press.

Spiegel, E. (2017). Managing stress for at-risk students. *Phi Delta Kappan, 98*(6), 42–46.

Stahnke, R., & Blömeke, S. (2021). Novice and expert teachers' situation-specific skills regarding classroom management: What do they perceive, interpret and suggest? *Teaching and Teacher Education, 98,* 103243. https://doi.org/10.1016/j.tate.2020.103243

Stellar, J. E., Cohen, A. B., Oveis, C., & Keltner, D. (2015). Affective and physiological responses to the suffering of others: Compassion and vagal activity. *Journal of Personality and Social Psychology, 108*(4), 572–585.

Tate, M. (2016). *Worksheets don't grow dendrites.* Corwin.

Texas Education Agency. (2021). *TEA releases spring 2021 STAAR Grades 3-8 and end-of-course assessment results; Outcomes for in-person learners appreciably higher than for those who were remote.* https://tea.texas.gov/about-tea/news-and-multimedia/news-releases/news-2021/tea-releases-spring-2021-staar-grades-3-8-and-end-of-course-assessment-results-outcomes-for-in-person-learners-appreciably-higher-than-for-those-who-were-remote

Trzeciak, S., & Mazzarelli, A. (2019). *Compassionomics: The revolutionary scientific evidence that caring makes a difference.* Studer Group.

Tyner, A. (2021). *How to sell SEL: Parents and the politics of social-emotional learning.* Thomas B. Fordham Institute. fordhaminstitute.org/how-to-sell-sel

Urick, A., Carpenter, B. W., & Eckert, J. (2021). Confronting COVID: Crisis leadership, turbulence, and self-care. *Frontiers in Education, 6,* 72. https://doi.org/10.3389/feduc.2021.642861

Van Der Kolk, B. (2014). *The body keeps the score.* Penguin.

Wiggins, G. (2012). Seven keys to effective feedback. *Educational Leadership, 70*(1), 10–16.

Wiggins, G., & McTighe, J. (2005). *Understanding by design* (Version 2, 2nd ed.). [Computer software]. Association for Supervision and Curriculum Design.

Will, M. (2021, January 6). As teacher morale hits a new low, schools look for ways to give breaks, restoration. *Education Week.* https://www.edweek.org/leadership/as-teacher-morale-hits-a-new-low-schools-look-for-ways-to-give-breaks-restoration/2021/01

Willingham, D. T. (2009). *Why don't students like school?* Jossey-Bass.

Yeager, D. S., Purdie-Vaughns, V., Garcia, J., Apfel, N., Brzustoski, P., Master, A., Hessert, W. T., Williams, M. E., & Cohen, G. L. (2014). Breaking the cycle of mistrust: Wise interventions to provide critical feedback across the racial divide. *Journal of Experimental Psychology: General, 143*(2), 804–824. https://doi.org/10.1037/a0033906

Index

A SAGE Publishing Company

Helping educators make the greatest impact

CORWIN HAS ONE MISSION: to enhance education through intentional professional learning.

We build long-term relationships with our authors, educators, clients, and associations who partner with us to develop and continuously improve the best evidence-based practices that establish and support lifelong learning.

Confident Teachers, Inspired Learners

CORWIN

CARLA MARSCHALL, ELIZABETH O. CRAWFORD

Nurture "Worldwise Learners": students who both deeply understand and purposefully act when learning about global challenges.

JULIE STERN, KRISTA FERRARO, KAYLA DUNCAN, TREVOR ALEO

Harness the critical concepts of traditional disciplines while building students' capacity to transfer their learning to solve novel and complex modern problems.

CHASE NORDENGREN

Demonstrate goal setting as an integral instructional strategy to help students take ownership of their learning.

JOHN HATTIE, DOUGLAS FISHER, NANCY FREY, SHIRLEY CLARKE

Working with other people can be a powerful accelerator of student learning and a precursor to future success.

To order your copies, visit **corwin.com/teachingessentials**

No matter where you are in your professional journey, Corwin aims to ease the many demands teachers face on a daily basis with accessible strategies that benefit ALL learners.

CAROL PELLETIER RADFORD

Equip teachers with the tools they need to take care of themselves so they can serve their students, step into leadership, and contribute to the education profession.

STEPAN MEKHITARIAN

Combine the best of distance learning and classroom instruction with a new vision for learning and professional development that capitalizes on the distance learning experience.

**SERENA PARISER,
VICTORIA S. LENTFER**

Find actionable answers to your most pressing questions on how to create and sustain dynamic classroom.

**STEPHANIE SMITH BUDHAI,
KRISTINE S. LEWIS GRANT**

Help teachers pivot instruction to ensure equitable, inclusive learning experiences in online and in-person settings.